The Book of Letters

How to write a letter for every occasion

R E V I S E D   E D I T I O N

Peter Breen

Illustrated by Ron Tandberg

To the memory of
David Piper (1944–1984)
and for Jennifer, Kate and Andrew

First published in 1986
This edition published in 2002

Allen & Unwin
83 Alexander Street
Crows Nest NSW 2065
Australia
Phone: (61 2) 8425 0100
Fax: (61 2) 9906 2218
Email: info@allenandunwin.com
Web: www.allenandunwin.com

National Library of Australia
Cataloguing-in-Publication entry:

Breen, Peter (Peter J.).
  The book of letters: how to write a letter for every
  occasion.

  3rd ed.
  Bibliography.
  Includes index.
  ISBN 1 86508 669 X.

  1. Commercial correspondence. 2. Letter writing.
  I. Tandberg, Ron, 1943– . II. Title.

Text design by Simon Paterson
Set in Janson Text 10/13 pt by Bookhouse, Sydney
Printed in Australia by McPherson's Printing Group

10 9 8 7 6 5 4 3 2 1

Contents

About the author

Peter Breen MLC is an independent member of the Upper House of the New South Wales Parliament. He represents the cross-bench on the parliament's Law and Justice Committee and the Committee on the Office of the Ombudsman and the Police Integrity Commission. He has served as Chairman of the Parliamentary Privileges and Ethics Committee, and as a member of the Joint Parliamentary Committee on Victims Compensation.

Peter is a former New South Wales Chairman of the Australian Small Business Association and he has practised as a solicitor and barrister since 1973. In 1993 he was senior projects officer, human rights, with Queensland's Electoral and Administrative Review Commission, a statutory body set up following the Fitzgerald Inquiry into Police Corruption. The inquiry recommended a statutory Bill of Rights for Queensland.

In 1999 Peter successfully moved for an inquiry by the New South Wales Parliament into a statutory Bill of Rights for New South Wales. He is currently preparing a report for the parliament on the results of the inquiry. Peter is the author of *Advance Australia Fair: Reforming the Legal System with a Rights and Responsibilities Code*, as well as previous editions of *The Book of Letters*, and *Holding the Dream: HomeFund Lessons for Home Buyers*.

Preface to the revised edition

When this little book was first published by Allen & Unwin in 1986, it included about 100 letters I frequently used in my law practice. The letters were useful to the extent that they provided a simple solution to a few common legal problems. Since then my letters database has expanded to more than 3000 letters stored on a computer program known as 'WriteQuick'. Further information about the WriteQuick program is included in the postscript to the new edition of the book.

Members of parliament have always been required to write vast numbers of letters on behalf of their constituents. We also engage in private correspondence on a range of issues from promoting good government to defending our expense allowances. Horace Walpole, a member of the British parliament in the eighteenth century, was one of the most prominent letter writers in the English language. His private correspondence of more than 3000 letters was published in 42 volumes.

Today, original letter writers abound, and several thousand letters is the annual output of many people I know, including local radio personality Alan Jones. A recent newspaper article about Jones described him as a one-man lobbying juggernaut whose letters make even the prime minister jump. Alan Jones is living proof that the art of letter writing is alive and well.

Part One of the new edition deals with the basic principles you need to know for effective letter writing. Good letters that hit the mark have four features you will soon recognise and emulate in your own correspondence. You will also learn how to address the person you are writing to and how to close your letters. It concludes with strategies you can employ to simplify letter writing including some hints about language.

Readers of earlier editions of the book will recognise letters for every occasion in Part Two. All the letters and the text have been updated, and a new section has been added to cover letters to government regulators. Some authorities deal with maladministration and corruption while others handle complaints about serious and substantial waste of public money.

One question I wanted to address in the new edition is the rapid expansion in the use of email, particularly since the September 11 attacks on the World Trade Centre in New York. Many of us, it seems, now prefer email to post because of the risk of chemical and biological agents turning up with our incoming correspondence. I have included a section on email and I argue that the important issue for letter writers is what we say, not the medium we use to say it.

As always, the book is intended to be a useful resource for small business operators and law consumers wishing to assert their rights, as well as general readers hoping to hone their letter writing skills. Few problems exist that the right letter will not go some way to solving. Even if it lightens the mood of a difficult situation, the letter will be effective. In the same vein, Ron Tandberg's cartoons are a welcome addition to the latest edition of the book, and I am grateful for his contribution.

My thanks also to Adriana Sammartano, John Dale, Mary Attard, Colin Enderby, David H. Lung, Beth Thomas, Mark David, J. Barry Anderson, Vicki Proudfoot, Ray Vella, Robert

Campbell, Gary Ward, Robyn Debreceny, Robert Breen, Valerie Armstrong, Vince Doyle, John McGee and Diane Thomas. I would especially like to thank Colette Vella and Sue Grose-Hodge at Allen & Unwin for editing and designing the book.

Peter Breen
Parliment House, Sydney
October 2001

Part One

HOW TO WRITE
EFFECTIVE LETTERS

Chapter One

The structure of effective letters

Four key features

People who write effective letters usually write with passion and to a plan. While most of us are passionate in our letters, writing to a plan may not be so simple. We need to begin with the four key features of effective letters:

- Person—Who are you writing to?
- Issue—What kind of letter are you writing?
- Purpose—What is the connection between the person you are writing to and the issue?
- Action—What kind of action do you want the person to take?

Every letter that makes an impact will include these four features. Needless to say, long letters can become unwieldy, and I would rarely write a letter of more than one or two pages.

Effective letters need to hold the attention of your reader regardless of the issue you are writing about. Good letter writers seem to be as comfortable on the subject of higher mathematics as they are with the weather forecast. Their secret is to stick like glue to the four key features, which are illustrated in Letter 1.1 to the State premier.

3

1.1   Key features letter

PERSON

The Hon. Robert Carr MP
Premier, Minister for the Arts, and Minister for Citizenship
Level 40, Governor Macquarie Tower
1 Farrer Place
SYDNEY NSW 2000

Dear Premier,

I refer to our brief discussion last week at the deputy ombudsman's book launch when I complimented you on the recent decision to preserve large areas of forest on the South Coast. This was a courageous decision in the face of tough opposition from the timber industry. You have created a lasting legacy for the people of New South Wales.

ISSUE

Another area of land I would like to see preserved for future generations is the Dharawal State Recreation Area on the edge of Campbelltown. I grew up in this area which is part of the O'Hares Creek Catchment located between Appin and Bulli.

Recently I inspected the site of a proposed rifle range and international shooting complex to be built smack bang in the middle of the Dharawal. Lee Rhiannon of the Greens also attended the inspection. A copy of a report in the local newspaper of our visit is attached.

PURPOSE

I know you were once interested in preserving the Dharawal by turning it into a national park. A newspaper article to that effect is enclosed. You are quoted as 'having a plan of ringing Sydney with a green rim of national parks'. Now is the time to act. Planning Minister Andrew Refshauge has taken control of the proposed development because of its regional significance. His decision is imminent.

ACTION

The Dharawal is an important link between the Royal National Park at Audley, the Southern Highlands and the Blue Mountains. Sydney could be literally surrounded by national parks if you were to act to protect the Dharawal. I fear that failing to act will mean that the Dharawal becomes overrun by the relentless expansion of Sydney to the south and the west.

Please give this matter your urgent and personal attention.

Yours sincerely,

P. Breen.

Peter Breen

Person

Letters are a form of communication and they need to focus on the person you are writing to. You will need to elicit some emotional response from the person if they are to take action on your behalf. Letters that focus on you, the writer, and not on the person you are writing to, will be ineffective. It may make you feel better to write the letter, but do not expect a meaningful response.

In Letter 1.1 to the premier, it would be quite futile to carry on about my horror and indignation at the prospect of a rifle range in an area of pristine wilderness. And it would be a complete waste of words to say I was shocked to the core at the destruction of the place of my childhood. The premier is more interested in the issue than how I feel, even though I may have a legitimate grievance. Forget about your own feelings and remain focused on the feelings of your correspondent.

What the premier wants to hear about is the good job he is doing to protect the environment. Any person you are writing to will respond only to the extent you strike a chord with something that interests them. In a complex world with wide ranging demands for our attention, our emotional responses are limited, and the issues that call us to action are the ones that stir passion. The worst thing you could do is write to the premier and ask him to stop trashing the environment.

Issue

Needless to say, an issue such as the environment has many aspects, and you need to be careful not to get sidetracked by the big picture. Concentrate on the details of the issue you are concerned about. It may be worth remembering the political slogan coined by the Greens—think globally and act locally. Nothing is so daunting on environmental issues than the magnitude of the problem.

Once you identify the issue, remain focused on it throughout the letter. You need to do your homework and find out about your correspondent's track record. If you use technical language that goes over the person's head, your letter is destined for the waste paper basket. Similarly, if your letter lectures the person or speaks down to them, you can expect a negative response.

In the example given, the premier's interest in the environment is well known—his government is supposed to be the greenest in Australia—and so it was a relatively simple task to refer to another of his projects and then make a connection with the environmental aspects of the rifle range proposal.

You will also need to demonstrate to the person your sensitivity to their interests and concerns, not just to your own. Communication is all about considering the needs of other people. It is not about sacrificing your own hopes and aspirations, but finding what you have in common with your correspondent and addressing that particular aspect of the issue.

Purpose

The purpose is the critical feature of your letter as it locks the person you are writing to into the issue you are concerned about. Your purpose may be related to your business or social life, or you may be seeking political or financial gain. Perhaps you want to influence a decision about the environment, or your purpose may be to support a charitable or community activity. The person you are writing to has some direct link with the issue and it is that link you want to exploit. A letter that hits the mark will literally strike at the heart of your correspondent.

The reason you are writing to a particular person about the issue reveals the purpose of your letter. Your purpose will determine the theme of your letter which we will look at in the next section. Essentially, the person you are writing to needs to have some first-hand experience of the issue if your letter is to get a positive response. Your letter should direct the attention of the person to this experience.

In the present example, a similar letter to the planning minister might be as effective as the letter to the premier provided you can identify a comparable commitment to protecting the environment. Again, the minister would need to be on the public record about the issue and your purpose would be to tie them down to this commitment. You are not seeking to shame the minister—rather, your aim is to appeal to their positive experience as the basis for the action you want.

Action

Effective letters generally conclude with a request for some positive action or response from the person you are writing to. If you are simply sharing information, include the benefits of that information in the closing paragraph of your letter. Be specific about the action or response you want and never assume that the reader will know what you have in mind.

It may be you want the person to take one of two alternative actions, such as replacing damaged goods or giving you a refund. State the alternatives clearly, otherwise your reader will find an excuse to put your letter to one side. If you are seeking a response to an invitation, make it clear how the person is to respond, the deadline and whether they can bring a partner.

The action you want may or may not include a response to your letter, but if you are concerned about getting a response, say so in the concluding paragraph. In my letter to the premier, I did not seek a response as I felt that the government was already in a difficult position on the issue. I did ask for action, however, and I am pleased to say that the government is now looking at an alternative site for the rifle range and shooting complex.

Finding the right theme

The central idea or message in your letter is the theme. It usually expresses some aspect of the human condition, particularly in letters demanding action from your correspondent. Finding the right theme is to understand the purpose of your letter. If you are to touch the heart of the person you are writing to, you will need to find the human experience that moves the person to action.

Unlike writing a novel, letter writing does not allow you the luxury of developing characters and a plot in order to promote your theme or message. On the bright side, even a modest letter will generally include some general observation about the human condition. You might want to write about individual liberty and freedom, the right to life, the pursuit of happiness, the quest for love, the eradication of evil or the importance of self-discovery. Each of these experiences can be reduced to a three or four paragraph letter.

Most importantly, the theme of your letter, like any appeal to the human heart, needs to be subtle. If you attempt to beat your correspondent over the head with bold statements about human rights, accountability or injustice, you will almost certainly render them senseless and incapable of responding to your letter. Again, it needs to be said that letter writing is about communication—focusing on the person you are writing to.

Recently I voted in the parliament against a bill that was supposed to keep one of the state's most notorious killers in gaol. I believed that the bill was fatally flawed and would have achieved the exact opposite of its intention, affording the prisoner an unexpected opportunity for release. Admittedly, the flaw in the bill raised a complex question of law, but all the leading lights of the legal profession confirmed the flaw. On this basis I opposed the bill. Reactions to the way I voted varied from horror to indignation as the bill was defeated by just one vote.

Compare extracts from two of the many letters I received about my vote on the bill. Letter 1.2 emphasises my needs whereas Letter 1.3 focuses on the writer's needs.

1.2 Recipient-focused letter

Dear Mr Breen,

I realise that the life sentences bill may be inconsistent with your human rights platform. Nevertheless, the safety of the community is also an important issue and one I expected you to support. For this reason I was very disappointed in the way you voted on the bill. Criminals like ... cannot be allowed to destroy the lives of innocent people. Perhaps you would be kind enough to inform me of the reasons for your decision as I am considering whether to withdraw my support from your party.

1.3 Writer-focused letter

Dear Mr Breen,

Please find enclosed formal resignation by my wife and myself from your Reform the Legal System Party. We are both ashamed that we have been associated with you because of your vote in the House on the life sentences bill. The killer is a monster who committed heinous crimes and you know it. If the way you voted is your idea of legal reform, you are obviously incompetent, mad or both. I find your actions disgusting in the extreme. Please do us the courtesy of removing our names from your mailing list.

Clearly the writer of Letter 1.3 wanted to vent his spleen and he had no real interest in communicating with me about the issue. I call this a 'rocket' letter as it is designed to explode on impact. The writer obviously did not wish to receive a reply. In fact no amount of work on my part was going to persuade the writer of this letter to change his mind, and it goes without saying that the right to hold an opinion includes the right to express that opinion in a letter.

The writer of Letter 1.2 on the other hand has the same concerns about the way I voted on the bill and so the reasons for my decision were important enough to seek a reply. This writer wanted communication and not confrontation. In effect, I was being offered the opportunity to explain my vote and the writer of the letter was deferring judgment until I provided the explanation. I was prompted by the tone of this letter to explain my decision in great detail and to forward copies of documents that supported my position.

So far as effective letters are concerned, it is possible to identify three broad themes in your correspondence. Other themes exist but most letters can be described as social, business or legal communications. Social letters deal with human gratitude, business letters concentrate on human achievement and legal letters emphasise human anxiety. These three themes can be illustrated in an acceptance letter.

Social

A social acceptance letter is a communication that begins with gratitude and usually concludes with words of praise for your correspondent. Make sure a letter addressed to two people refers to your friend or family member in the correct order—friends and family go first, followed by the names of other people. The idea that a husband's name should appear before the name of his spouse is one consigned to history, along with the idea that a woman's title should describe her marital status. Some women prefer the title 'Mrs' to 'Ms' and in these cases it would be offensive to ignore their wishes and use the latter form of address.

Letter 1.4 was written in response to an invitation from one of my five sisters and her husband asking me to attend the wedding of my niece.

1.4   Social acceptance letter

Margaret and Gary Ward
123 Ward Street
Wardville STA 22422

Dear Margaret and Gary,

I was delighted to receive your invitation to Simone's wedding on Saturday 18 November at the University of Sydney followed by a reception at the Royal Motor Yacht Club. It will be a splendid affair and my great pleasure to attend.

Might I also say that the David Jones gift card accompanying the invitation is a wonderful idea. I expect to have the opportunity in the next few days to visit the David Jones store in the city to inspect the gift suggestions made by Simone and her fiancé.

I am very excited about the wedding and I know the family is looking forward to the celebration. You were very thoughtful to choose a date when we are all available and we love you dearly for it.

Yours sincerely,

Peter

Peter

Gratitude and praise are themes easily identified in this letter. I was grateful for the invitation and I wanted to express my thanks to my sister and her husband for sending it to me. In this particular letter, the middle paragraph includes a reference to the wishes of my niece regarding gift selection. You will always find some unique aspect of a social invitation worthy of a compliment in your reply and the opportunity to say something positive should not be missed.

Some people use writing paper and personal stationery to handwrite social letters, or even plain white cards when accepting a personal invitation, but it is less common in a world of computer-generated correspondence. Personal touches these days are found most commonly in the email symbols of cyberspace. Retaining the personal touch in your social correspondence is important, however, and one way to be sure you conclude your letter on the right theme is to confirm your love, admiration and regard for your correspondent.

Business

Although less intimate than social letters, business letters never-theless require your personal signature, and therefore some element of your personality will be conveyed in what you say. The most common theme in business letters is shared achievement. Even when communicating bad news, the effective business letter will include some positive reference to common objectives and goals. Letter 1.5 is a business acceptance letter whose aspirational theme stands in contrast to the intimacy of the comparable social letter.

1.5   Business acceptance letter

Mr Jack Ho Chan
Computer Programmer
Ace Software Design
21 Microchip Drive
Cybervalley STA 29888

Dear Jack,

Thank you for sending me the quote for enhancements to the WriteQuick letter writing system.

You did not specifically include in the quote the cost of updating the 3000 letters in the database and I assume it is a simple process from a programming point of view. Provided my assumption is correct, and updating the letters will not require an inordinate amount of time, I accept the quote.

One issue that does require further discussion is the difficulty many people experience when they attempt to access the program using Internet Explorer. I know you are aware of the problem and I look forward to any suggestions you might have to help those of us who are technically challenged users.

I am returning the CD-ROM prototype as requested so that you can forward it to Sony Corporation for a production costing. I have taken the liberty of suggesting a couple of changes to the copy on the plastic cover as well as the disk itself. The proposed changes are written on the attached photocopy pages.

I understand that you will be making changes to the installation instructions. Please note that the user needs to acknowledge the attached draft licence. Perhaps an additional item under 'First Things First' would be appropriate.

I look forward to hearing from you and trust that the success we have enjoyed to date will continue into the next phase of the project.

Yours sincerely,

P. Breen.

Peter Breen

People writing business letters generally stick to the bare essentials, deliberately avoiding the warm and fuzzy themes of social letters, and concentrating on the common business goals they share with their correspondents. One reason may be the legitimate concerns we all have about mixing business and social activities. Another problem with business letters that stray into the excessively personal themes is they somehow lack credibility. This may be an idiosyncrasy on my part, of course, but the acid test is how you would feel about your letter being read out in court.

Over the years I have seen business people cringe with embarrassment on numerous occasions when their excessively personal letters were tendered in court in the context of a business dispute. Even generous praise for a business colleague may be a disaster if it subsequently becomes necessary to defend yourself against a claim by the person. I am reminded of the long list of court cases over personal references, written with the best will in the world, and subsequently used as the basis for a claim that the glowing remarks about a person are wrong, and somebody has relied on those remarks to their detriment. Many people in business will not write a personal reference for fear of being sued over the expectations created by the reference. Further information on this subject is included in Chapter Fifteen.

For all that, it is neither possible nor desirable to avoid all personal themes in your correspondence. My advice is to confine and refine your remarks if you want to avoid trying to justify them out of context. Obvious exaggerations and excessive language may be acceptable in advertising, but not in letter writing, with the exception, perhaps, of 'rocket' letters and sales and marketing letters. The secret is to choose the personable phrase over the excessively personal one, such as 'I am grateful for your advice' instead of 'Once again you have rescued me'.

Legal

Human anxiety is the general theme of legal letters and for that reason it is often good practice to consult an expert if your letter raises serious legal questions. While doctors deliver babies and make you well, it needs to be said that lawyers deliver briefs that often make you sick, and most members of the legal profession have a good deal of experience in the field of human anxiety. Nevertheless, a lawyer's letter carries some weight in the mind of the recipient. You must decide, therefore, whether this added weight to your letter is sufficient to justify the lawyer's fee.

Legal letters have no defining characteristic except perhaps that people presume they represent an authoritative statement on a particular issue. You need to distinguish between a lawyer's letter and a legal letter. If you look up the law on a problem and then write a letter about it, you are the author of a legal letter. You may consult a lawyer if you wish, but if you write the letter it remains your copyright property, even if you quote the lawyer's advice.

Many people write legal letters without consulting a lawyer, and the legal acceptance letter, for example, frequently appears under corporate or personal letterheads. Given a choice between a lawyer's letter and writing my own legal letter on private or business letterhead, I would choose the latter. Somehow a lawyer's letter is too confronting, particularly in a business situation where you might be building a co-operative relationship. Lawyers always talk about the 'other side' in their correspondence, an expression that bears all the hallmarks of human anxiety. If you want to minimise this theme in your legal correspondence, use Letter 1.6 as a guide and write on private letterhead.

1.6   Legal acceptance letter

Ms I. N. Dent
81 Parramatta Road
Dodge City STA 27999

Dear Ms Dent,

As requested, I am enclosing two repair quotations for the damage to my motor vehicle, one from the repairer nominated by you and the other from Big Bang Smash Repairs. I note that both quotes total about $1200 and you accept full responsibility for payment of the damage.

You indicated you need three months to pay on the basis that you have arranged to go overseas for the next six weeks. When you return, you will need a further period of six weeks to save up the $1200.

Rather than pay by instalments, you would prefer to make one payment of the amount due.

I am quite satisfied with this arrangement. With your permission I will contact you in three months' time and arrange to collect a cheque for $1200. I realise how difficult it is to meet unexpected expenses and I remain grateful that nobody was injured in the accident.

Yours sincerely,

A Bush Lawyer

A. Bush-Lawyer (Mr)

Written acceptance of a payment arrangement, quote or other form of offer has wider implications in the context of a legal letter than a social or business acceptance letter. A letter accepting a quote, for example, is legally binding from the moment your

correspondent receives the letter. In order to make a binding contract you need offer, acceptance and consideration, and a lawyer will be happy to write the letter for you using the correct terminology and jargon. But there is no reason why you should not write the letter yourself and I can think of many positive reasons why you might consider taking pen in hand.

One obvious reason for the do-it-yourself letter is the cost saving. Another reason is that your own letter is actually more flexible than the lawyer's letter. By this I mean you can afford to be a bit vague if you write the letter yourself and this may be no bad thing if a dispute arises. For example, acceptance of the payment arrangement in Letter 1.6 deliberately avoids threats and sanctions to allow room for further negotiation, if the person is unable to pay. A lawyer's letter is unlikely to include conciliatory language of this kind.

Setting the right tone

The tone of your letter is the spirit in which you communicate your theme or message. You may be feeling sarcastic, cynical, anxious, humorous or argumentative when you draft the letter. If so, I would discard the letter and try again when your mood changes. Setting one of these tones is fraught with danger for most of us. Generally it will be safer to stick to one or the other of the established tones: formal or informal, positive or negative, polite or 'rocket' and personal or impersonal.

Formal or informal

Social letters may be formal or informal, depending upon the occasion and how well you know your correspondent. Recently

I received an informal letter from another of my sisters on the occasion of her husband's birthday.

1.7   Informal letter

Dear Peter,

Roy turns 50 on Saturday 10 September and we would love you to join us for a bit of a bash at our place. We will light the barbecue about 6 p.m. Bring a salad or dessert plate, and booze, but we will look after the meat for the barbecue.

The family bought Roy a new set of golf clubs and you are welcome to contribute $50. Otherwise, a present is unnecessary.

Ring and let us know if you can make it.

Love,

Janette

Janette

A formal letter is appropriate for state, academic and business functions, or formal occasions such as weddings and funerals. Just prior to the 2000 Olympics the lord mayor of Sydney sent me a formal letter.

1.8   Formal letter

Dear Mr Breen,

You are invited to a Civic Reception in honour of the International Olympic Family on Thursday 14 September 2000 at 5 p.m. at Sydney Town Hall.

All guests will be subject to security checks upon arrival at the Town Hall. Please ensure you arrive in good time to avoid entrance delays as large crowds are expected in George Street.

Road closures in George Street are in effect from 4.30 p.m. as a result of the Torch Arrival Ceremony and vehicular access will be restricted.

Yours sincerely,

for Frank Sartor

Frank Sartor
Lord Mayor of Sydney

Positive or negative

In an ideal world all letters would promote a positive theme or message. Think and write on the bright side, even when you are communicating bad news. Concentrate on the needs of your correspondent and put yourself in their position. Would *you* want to read a letter designed to disappoint and depress you, or would you prefer to read about the positive aspects of a difficult situation?

Sometimes it will be necessary to adopt a negative tone in your letter, such as a reply to a mischievous or misconceived request. Nobody can meet everyone's expectations and in these cases it is best to say—in the nicest way possible—you cannot assist. Certainly you should not be offensive or use an alienating tone in your reply. Say what must be said without being pejorative or didactic, but say it in a way that the person will know your door is closed on this particular issue.

Polite or 'rocket'

Again, the general rule is that you should strive to be polite in your letters. A polite letter will rarely get you into trouble and, in your own small way, you will make the world a more civilised place for all of us. If you decide to send a 'rocket', however, you will want to be as rude as possible without descending to common abuse. I wrote Letter 1.9 to my neighbour after his barking dog drove me to make a declaration of war.

1.9   'Rocket' letter

Mr Richard Cranium
27 Peaceful Place
Scenic Hills STA 26333

Dear Richard,

Last night your barking dog just about sent me round the bend. I told you about it this morning and you offered to let me pat the dog. As I mentioned, I pat the bloody thing over the fence all the time, hoping to settle it down.

You are the problem, not the dog. Anyone who chops wood, plays loud music and feeds his dog at three o'clock in the morning has no regard for the sleeping arrangements of his neighbours. Your dog's bad habits, I suspect, are merely a reflection of your own inconsiderate behaviour.

You said the dog does not disturb you at night. One reason might be your bedroom is located at the front of your house while the dog seems to have marked out its territory along the back fence, adjacent to my bedroom window. If you were to confine the dog at night, perhaps in the vicinity of your own bedroom, you may have some small understanding of my agitation.

Please regard this letter as a declaration of war. I intend taking my complaint to the police, local council, the chamber magistrate and the local member of parliament. Your barking dog is a church mouse compared to the noise I can make.

If the war goes your way and I am forced to move, I will sue you for relocation expenses, loss of the amenity of my residence and post traumatic stress disorder, not to mention the costs of my lawyer, who charges like the light brigade, and sends cruise missiles instead of rocket letters.

Yours sincerely,

P. Breen.

Peter Breen

As it happened, I did not send this letter—not immediately, anyway. First, I checked on the dog owner's responsibility under the Dog Act to make sure I was on solid ground with my complaint. Then I approached the police and local council and discovered that complaints about dogs can be addressed by submitting a special form to the council. I filled out the form and the authorities knocked on my neighbour's door. But that was all they could do, and when the situation failed to improve, I sent the letter. The dog now sleeps on the verandah of the house, in close proximity to my neighbour's bedroom, and it rarely barks at night for fear of disturbing its master.

For all the apparent success of this missive, relations with my neighbour were never quite the same after sending a rocket letter. Exhaust your other remedies before writing to your neighbour as this is a measure of last resort. Dialogue is the best way to deal with a neighbourhood dispute because the written word has a nasty habit of escalating emotions. A rocket letter inevitably means an explosion and you will want to be as far removed as possible from the fallout. You cannot avoid it if you live next door.

Personal or impersonal

In all your correspondence try to use a conversational tone—as if a real person were talking. Try reading your letter aloud and

YOU GOT MY LETTER?

imagine the person you are writing to is listening to your voice. Remember, a letter is a form of communication, and the effective letter is one that involves dialogue. Make sure you write the way you speak, using words you normally use and expressing ideas that represent your own view of how the world goes around. One sure way to check the personal tone in your letter is to look for the personal pronouns 'I' and 'we' and 'you'. Compare the personal Letter 1.10 with the impersonal Letter 1.11.

1.10 Personal letter

Dear Peter,

Last Thursday we had a very successful meeting of the Reform the Legal System Party. Most of the members turned up and listened with great interest to the guest speaker, Dr Bill Bloggs. He is an absorbing character whose ideas about law reform gave us much to think about.

We missed your inappropriate interjections and good humour, and hope you can make the next meeting. You may be interested in the attached copy of the draft minutes, although they need to be checked by Alistair.

A question was raised at the meeting about your level of involvement with the party. We know you have a lot on your plate, but some members feel you need to be doing more to raise our public profile. What do you think about that?

1.11 Impersonal letter

Dear Mr Breen,

Last Thursday's meeting of the Reform the Legal System Party was well attended. The guest speaker was interesting.

Minutes of the meeting are attached and the absence of several executive members was noted. Apologies might have been in order. In due course, the secretary will check the minutes, hopefully in time for the next meeting.

At this stage the key stakeholders in law reform need to be doing more to give the party a higher public profile. There is nothing personal in these remarks, which are consistent with a resolution of the meeting, and further details are to be found in the minutes.

Combining different tones

Earlier, I described the tone of your letter as the spirit in which you communicate your theme. Hopefully, you will appeal to the heart of the person you are writing to through your tone, but people have complex emotions, and it is likely that the same letter will include more than one tone. Above all, the tones you choose will need to be believable if you are to strike a heart chord with your correspondent. Also, you can be sure that the way you feel will be revealed in the tone of your letter, so you may want to put off writing while you feel angry or disappointed. If your letter is unrelievedly insulting, excessively flattering or demanding in its tone, you are unlikely to elicit a meaningful response.

Any narrow, one-dimensional tone will immediately lack credibility because we are not like that in real life. Nobody can take seriously a string of insults or demands. The same goes with excessive flattery. What you say cannot be taken at face value because it does not seem to be sincere. However, sincerity also has its pitfalls—what you are doing is focusing your attention on your own needs instead of the needs of your correspondent. I am not denying the need to be sincere in your letters, but communication is a process of finding common ground and shared interests.

You are more likely to find the emotion that resonates with your reader if you try different tones in your letter. For example, even an insulting letter can include some redeeming quality such as a change of tone. You have a better chance of being taken seriously if you direct a series of insults to a person but at the same time add humour, pathos or the possibility of reconciliation. Make your letter light and dark, clear and opaque, rough and smooth, and its sincerity will speak for itself. Effective letters bear all the hallmarks of the human condition, and their tones are many and varied.

In the next chapter we will look at the formal parts of a letter, how to begin with the correct salutation, how to close and what you need to include in your letter to make it do the job. Your letter is an integrated and crafted piece of narrative—a work of art—and it will literally write itself if the important elements in the story are allowed to unfold. We will look also at the correct forms of address and salutation in your letters, whether you are writing a personal letter to a friend, or a formal letter to a government or diplomatic official.

Chapter Two

The formalities

Formal parts of a letter

It is worth remembering the formal parts of a letter even if you use email for most of your correspondence. You never know when you will need a formal letter to make a presentation or score a job. Most letters include many or all of the following formal parts:

- letterhead or heading
- date and personal line
- inside address
- salutation
- reference line
- body
- complimentary close
- signature block
- postscript and enclosures.

During the Sydney 2000 Olympic and Paralympic Games I found myself trying to explain to numerous visitors to Australia why we have the Union Jack in the corner of the Australian flag. After the games I decided to write to the governor-general about my difficulties. Letter 2.1 is the letter I sent him and it illustrates the formal parts of a letter.

2.1 Formal parts letter

HEADING

Parliament House
Macquarie Street
Sydney NSW 2000

DATE AND PERSONAL LINE

PERSONAL   1 July 2001

INSIDE ADDRESS

His Excellency The Right Rev. Dr Peter Hollingworth AC OBE
Governor-General of the Commonwealth of Australia
Government House
Dunrossil Drive
YARRALUMLA ACT 2600

SALUTATION

Dear Governor-General,

REFERENCE LINE

Re: The Australian Flag

BODY

May I offer my warmest congratulations on your appointment as governor-general. I am a longstanding admirer of your work for the underprivileged, and your exemplary record in community service speaks for itself.

I believe you are also uniquely placed to do something about the Union Jack in the corner of the Australian flag. As the Queen's representative in Australia, and a senior member of the Anglican Church, it seems to me you get two bites of the cherry, so to speak.

You might have noticed that no representation of the Union Jack appeared on the Australian team uniforms at either the Olympics or Paralympics. Perhaps this was intentional, to avoid confusing the English spectators.

Mind you, numerous Australian competitors proudly wore the Southern Cross on their tracksuits and sportswear, and I was struck by the idea that the Southern Cross on its own would do quite nicely as a symbol of Australia on our flag.

If you have the opportunity to discuss British symbols in Australia with the Queen I will be exceedingly grateful. Removing the Union Jack from the Australian flag would be a small change to the way we are governed and a fitting way to celebrate the Centenary of Federation.

CLOSE

Yours sincerely,

SIGNATURE BLOCK

P. Breen.

Peter Breen

POSTSCRIPT

PS   Please avoid raising the matter of the flag with the prime minister, who is likely to offer us a choice between the flag as it is and a hessian bag on a stick if the republic referendum is any guide.

Letterhead or heading

If you place your address at the top of the letter, either to the right or left of the page, this is called the heading. Traditionally, the heading appears just above the date. If you add your name and other details such as telephone and fax numbers, you have a letterhead. You could centre the letterhead on the page and add details of your business or profession. Also, you may want to include a graphic. Make sure your letterhead looks professional and conveys a positive message about you and your business.

Following are two examples of the kinds of letterhead you can create using the WriteQuick program.

BROWNSVILLE
STEEL COMPANY

steel for the new millennium
321 BROWN STREET BROWNSVILLE NSW 2530 AUSTRALIA

TEL: 9765 4321 FAX: 9765 4320
mbrown@brownsteel.com.au   www.brownsteel.com.au

JONES HILL TRAVEL
COMPANY LIMITED

world travel specialists

654 JONES STREET JONES HILL QUEENSLAND
All Correspondence to
PO BOX 456 JONES HILL QLD 4570
TEL: 7765 4321 FAX: 7765 4320
mjones@joneshilltravel.com.au   www.joneshilltravel.com.au

Certain symbols of a profession or business may be used as graphics in your letterhead. In the law we frequently use the scales of justice (although the sword of Damocles might be more appropriate). Once I paid a graphics company close to $1000 for a couple of pen strokes I considered using as a logo. In the end I, however, stuck with the traditional scales of justice. Simple graphics are fashionable but you also run the risk in Australia of being too cute by half. Whichever way you choose, if you are in business for the long haul, you will want to be recognised in the market place, and registering your corporate logo as a trade-mark is one way to protect your investment. You can pick up an application kit for a trademark from IP Australia (formerly the Office of Patents, Trademarks and Designs) in your local capital city.

Dateline

Most computer-generated letters include the date as an automatic function. It may be on the right or left of the page, usually below the heading. People using letterhead or personal stationery often insert the date immediately above the inside address, on the left of the page. Personally, I like to see the date at the right of the page where it is clearly visible on its own.

Sometimes a time lag between the writing of a letter and its signing and despatch will be indicated by a date stamp at the end of a letter, immediately below the signature. Ministers and government officials frequently employ this method of inserting a date. Usually they will date stamp the letter as they sign it. The pitfall with this method of dating a letter is that the delay will often mean events have overtaken the letter.

A surprising number of letters are not dated, whether by omission or because of the misconceived idea that a date restricts the application of certain correspondence such as a circular letter. Large mailings cannot always be processed in one or two days, and so a person may think it is a clever ploy not to date the letter. This is a big mistake. Anybody with direct marketing experience will tell you that undated letters are consigned to the rubbish bin.

Personal line

Immediately opposite the dateline is the place to insert a warning that this letter is personal, private or confidential. Use bold letters so that the note catches the eye of the person who opens the letter who may not be the same person as your correspondent. If you only intend your letter to be read by the person you are writing to, say so in bold letters and using words such as 'Personal' or 'Private' or 'Confidential'. You must do this if you attack a person's integrity, beliefs or reputation in a letter, otherwise you will be exposing yourself to an action in damages for defamation (see Chapter Four).

The problem with publishing defamatory material in a letter is you can never be sure who will read what you have to say. If you say something nasty about a person in a letter, and the letter is opened by the person's secretary or personal assistant, immediately you are in trouble. For this reason the personal line should appear on the envelope as well as on your letter. Some people are extremely cautious about publishing defamatory letters and go so far as to write on the envelope words such as 'To be opened by addressee only'.

Computer-generated correspondence such as emails raise particular difficulties if you want to say something nasty. Unlike personal correspondence sent by post, an email is not secure, and you could easily defame somebody if a number of people can access the email. To this extent the words 'Personal' or 'Private' or 'Confidential' may not protect you if you say something defamatory in an email.

One way to avoid the problem is to send an email attachment. Provided you warn the person in the email that the attachment is a horror letter and should be deleted once it is read, you are unlikely to be held accountable for any subsequent publication of the letter. Alternatively, you can save the document with a password and notify your correspondent of the password in a way that ensures the security of what you have written.

Usually, you can be more damning of politicians than other people in your letters because our elected representatives are expected to withstand a greater degree of public scrutiny than the rest of the community. Here is a letter I received after making a comment that the United States Constitution gave the American people the right to vote but not the right to have their vote counted. Note that the letter included the word 'Confidential' on the date line, as the author originally intended the letter for my eyes only. Subsequently we spoke about the issues raised in the letter and the author agreed to its publication.

2.2   Confidential letter

CONFIDENTIAL

Dear Mr Breen,

Once again I hear you pushing the idea that Australia needs a Bill of Rights. This time you are quoting the result of the US presidential election to promote your ridiculous notion. Surely the 5–4 decision of the US Supreme Court along political lines to install George W. Bush as President proves conclusively that a Bill of Rights politicises the judiciary.

Australia already has the 1689 Bill of Rights and the common law which have served us well. We also have electoral laws that guarantee the right to vote. This nonsense you are spreading that Australia is the only common law country that does not have a Bill of Rights is false and misleading.

It may suit you as a lawyer to have judges deciding political questions, but because judges are unelected, they are unreliable representatives of the will of the people. You also fail to understand that people loathe the legal system, and while a Bill of Rights is likely to generate more work for lawyers, it will be a disaster for the rest of us as we troop off to court to claim our legal rights.

Yours faithfully,

John Hewitt

Politicians do not enjoy the same freedom in their correspondence that attaches to their speeches in parliament. Parliamentary privilege is restricted to utterances in the House and people rightly expect politicians to be fully accountable for what they say elsewhere. For this reason—and also because of the importance of communication—I would not take anybody to task for their political opinion in a letter, even though I might hold a strong contrary view. My reply to the above letter was a measured response even though I am passionate about the need for a Bill of Rights.

2.3   Confidential reply

CONFIDENTIAL

Dear Mr Hewitt,

You were very kind to write to me about the Bill of Rights issue. I agree with you that the American Bill of Rights has politicised the United States Supreme Court, but I would not for one minute suggest that the American model is the kind of Bill of Rights we need in Australia. What we need is a statutory Bill of Rights along the lines of the English Human Rights Act recently passed by the British Parliament.

A modern statutory Bill of Rights (as opposed to the American constitutional model) actually diminishes the power of unelected judges. The English model, for example, requires a judge to refer back to parliament any question of interpretation inconsistent with the intention of the Human Rights Act. In other words, decisions about fundamental questions of human rights are to be made by the parliament, not judges. This is consistent with the doctrine of parliamentary supremacy that lies at the heart of the Westminster system of government.

Judges and lawyers enjoy too much power in our legal system, as you rightly point out, but I believe this is changing. With 30 per cent of litigants now unrepresented, courts are being forced to adapt to the needs of people who have no legal experience. Once court forms are made uniform and the law is placed on computer (with access for all people) the legal system will be greatly simplified.

It is to this end I suggest we need a statutory Bill of Rights codifying our basic rights and responsibilities. A simple statement of the fundamental principles underlying our democracy—a statutory Bill of Rights—would go a long way towards providing access to the legal system for ordinary people. Furthermore, a statutory Bill of Rights requires members of parliament to think twice about passing laws that breach important principles protecting the rights of citizens.

The New South Wales Parliament is currently examining the question of a statutory Bill of Rights and I will be pleased to provide any information from the inquiry that may interest you. Of course, you are free to attend hearings and seminars conducted by the inquiry, and a program is enclosed for your information.

Yours faithfully,

Peter Breen

Politicians in general are accustomed to tough correspondence. The trick is to say what you think without burning your bridges because issues come and go. Recently I wrote Letter 2.4 to the minister for roads. At the time I was taking advice about suing his government and so the letter was written on a 'Without Prejudice' basis.

2.4   'Without Prejudice' letter

WITHOUT PREJUDICE

The Hon. Carl Scully MP
Minister for Transport and Minister for Roads
Level 34, Governor Macquarie Tower
1 Farrer Place
SYDNEY NSW 2000

Dear Mr Scully,

I wrote to you earlier this year about the possibility of legal action over the failure of the Roads and Traffic Authority (RTA) to install filtration equipment in the M5 East Road Tunnel. You will recall I have made several submissions on behalf of the Residents Against Polluting Stacks (RAPS), who represent the people living in close proximity to the motor vehicle exhaust emissions stack attached to the road tunnel.

Since my last correspondence I had hoped that evidence gathered by the Upper House parliamentary inquiry would convince you of the need for filtration to protect the environment and the health of the local community. Following publication of the report of the inquiry in the last few weeks, however, I note with concern that the RTA has dismissed the findings out of hand.

Against all the evidence, the RTA still says either that the filtration equipment does not work, or that it is unnecessary. According to my information the authority is wrong on both counts. The legal proceedings I have foreshadowed will be won by whoever has the best scientific evidence on this issue, and I believe the RTA is on a hiding to nothing.

I am also informed that the cost of filtration equipment is now in the price range of $10 million. You will recall your undertaking to filter the exhaust emissions if the filtration equipment could be installed for this price and I am at a loss to know why you steadfastly refuse to act. The RTA estimates it will cost $37 million to retrofit the equipment once the tunnel is opened and, as expected, pollution levels are exceeded.

In the circumstances the local community has no alternative other than to commence court proceedings. I will not be involved personally in the proceedings, which will be conducted by the Environmental Defender's Officer, but if you would like me to arrange a meeting with RAPS at any time please feel free to contact me.

Yours sincerely,

Peter Breen

The expression 'Without Prejudice' frequently appears in the personal line. Strictly speaking, the expression is limited to correspondence between two litigants. If one party to legal proceedings writes a 'Without Prejudice' letter to the other party, usually offering to settle the proceedings, this means that the terms of the offer are not admissible as evidence if the litigation proceeds to a hearing. You can also use the expression before commencing proceedings to indicate you are willing to forgo your right to a legal remedy provided the dispute is resolved to your satisfaction.

Finally, the personal line is a useful place to mark your letter for the attention of a particular person. Sometimes you will want to write to a person in a government department or corporation but you don't know the person's position or title. In this case, address the letter to the director or general manager and simply include the name of your contact in the personal line. Letter 2.5 may be useful.

2.5 'For Attention' letter

Attention: Dr Joe Bloggs

General Manager
NSW Parliamentary Library
Parliament House
SYDNEY NSW 2000

Dear Dr Bloggs,

I am considering a private member's bill to deal with problems under the Defamation Act for Internet Service Providers (ISPs). You may be aware that ISPs are in a similar position to newsagents a few years ago when retailing defamatory material in newspapers was thought to be part of the publication process.

Similar questions arise today as to whether the ISPs are publishers or simply information carriers. ISPs have no prospect of policing the various Internet sites they host and they ought to be protected by an amendment to the defamation laws.

In the same vein, the common law defence of innocent publication might be given statutory recognition in the amendment. Senior counsel informs me that the common law defence at present is as follows:

> Although the general principle is that all persons who participate in a publication share in liability for that publication, a defence of 'innocent dissemination' is available at common law if any one of the participants is able to demonstrate that:
>
> i)   he or she did not know that the publication contained libel;
> ii) the ignorance was not due to negligence on his or her part; and
> iii) he or she had no ground for supposing that the publication was likely to contain defamatory material.

Any suggestions you have would be greatly appreciated. In particular I am anxious to know what Commonwealth and State defamation laws have to say about the liability of ISPs for defamatory material on the Internet.

Yours sincerely,

Peter Breen

Inside address

Most correspondence includes an inside address, which is simply the name, title, address and other details of the person you are writing to as the information appears on the letter. It is literally the address inside the envelope—as opposed to the address on the envelope itself. Usually both addresses will be the same, although some people insist you address them in a particular way and at a specific address. For example, recently I was informed by a constituent that I should stop sending her letters at her business address otherwise she would charge me for reading them.

If you have a mailing list stored on computer, the information is collected in database fields, and these fields will determine the inside address on your letters. Two popular programs are Microsoft Access and Filemaker Pro. Both give you great flexibility with your mailing list, and you will be limited only by the fields you choose when setting up the database. Allow for anomalies such as street addresses that are different from mailing addresses and include the maximum number of fields in your mailing list. Here is a sample of the fields you might want to use:

Title: Ms, Mr, Mrs, Dr, 'Blank', etc.
In your database 'Blank' means no title. The reason for this is that more and more people are dropping titles in their correspondence, particularly when writing emails.

First name: John, Mary, Bill, Joan, etc.
Make sure you leave sufficient room in this field for two names as a letter to Mr and Mrs Smith is often addressed to 'Mr John and Mrs Mary Smith', or simply 'John and Mary Smith'.

Second name: Smith, Jones, Brown, etc.
Again, you will need to allow for the possibility of two names in case you are writing to two people who share their lives but not their names. Your database fields should recognise 'Mr John Smith and Ms Mary Brown'.

Position: Director, Secretary, Chairman, etc.
Include gender-specific terms such as 'Chairwoman' and the gender neutral 'Chair' and 'Chairperson', although 'Chairman' is unfortunately probably correct most of the time.

Organisation: Company, Department, Club, etc.

Allow plenty of room in this field as some organisations have lengthy names to cover a multitude of interests and activities.

Address: 34 Smith Street, Post Office Box 111, etc.

Allow two lines for this field even though it normally requires just one line as some people use the name of their house or rural property in their address.

City/Suburb/Town: Smithfield, Jonesville, Browntown, etc.

One line is sufficient, but remember that the State and post-code will appear on the same line, so leave plenty of room if you intend using the same field.

State: New South Wales, Victoria, Queensland, etc.

It is important to include the abbreviation NSW, Vic, Qld, etc. in the database field to reduce the opportunity for error in a case where the suburb or town you are writing to is to be found in more than one State.

Postcode: 2000, 3000, 2600, etc.

A useful feature of some database programs is that the postcode is inserted automatically as soon as you key in the name of the suburb or town and State.

Punctuation in the inside address is a matter of personal preference and the rules are quite flexible. Today, we punctuate only when it is necessary and many letter writers do not use punctuation at all in the inside address. No punctuation is used in the inside address in the sample letters in the WriteQuick program, for example, although it is a matter of convenience more than anything else. Similarly, with email letters quite often we find no punctuation, particularly when an author writes large numbers of letters.

My own idiosyncrasies when it comes to punctuation in the inside address will be apparent from a quick review of the first letter at the beginning of this chapter. Some people prefer to use commas to separate initials signifying public office, honours and academic degrees when there is more than one of them. I like to place a full stop after a person's initials, and following an abbreviation of their title such as 'Hon.', 'Rev.', etc. Apart from those occasions, save your ink I say. What matters is the content of your letter and whether you manage to grab the attention of your reader.

Salutation

The correct way to address a person you do not know in a letter is quite different from meeting them personally. You can meet a person and immediately call them by their first name, unless they hold a particular academic, judicial or religious office, when you would call them 'Professor', 'Judge' or 'Bishop', for example. But if you write a letter to a person you do not know or you just

met, never address them by their first name. It is always 'Dear Ms Jones' or 'Dear Mr Smith' or 'Dear Bishop Thomas'.

If you are writing to a person who holds a particular public or religious office, you will need to decide whether your letter is formal or informal. You will need to make this decision whether or not you have met the person. For example, would you begin a letter to a judge with, 'Dear Judge Black' or 'Your Honour'? Would you address a bishop as 'Dear Bishop Thomas' or 'My Lord'? These questions are answered at the end of this chapter under the heading 'Forms of address'. Whether your letter is formal or informal, however, the important point needs to be repeated: you should not address *anybody* by their first name in a letter unless you know them personally.

Another point to remember when you address a person in a letter is to make sure the salutation is consistent with the inside address and the complimentary close. Again, 'familiarity' with your correspondent is of fundamental importance to your decision to write 'Dear Mary' or 'Dear Ms Jones', depending on how well you know the person. If you do not know Mary at all, the decision is simple: 'Ms Mary Jones' begins the inside address followed by the salutation 'Dear Ms Jones'. If you know Mary reasonably well you may begin 'Dear Mary'.

When writing to more than one woman, the French title Mesdames (Mses) may be used, or in the case of men, Messieurs (Messrs), although the expressions are increasingly uncommon, even in diplomatic and legal circles where they have been most popular. Correspondence to a husband and wife need not indicate the marital status of either of them, and should refer to them separately if they do not use the same name. Your inside address and salutation should begin with the name of the person you know best, either the wife or the husband. If you are related to one of them, that person's name should appear first. If you know the woman prefers to be addressed as 'Mrs' rather than 'Ms' then use that form, otherwise use 'Ms'.

Reference line

In the letter to the governor-general at the beginning of this chapter, the reference or subject line read 'Re: The Australian Flag'. I used the line to illustrate this feature of a letter, but it was probably unnecessary in the context of that particular letter because the subject is obvious in the first couple of paragraphs. It is common in legal and commercial correspondence to use a reference line, however, so that your correspondent can quickly identify the subject of your letter. This is important for people who receive vast amounts of correspondence, and for similar reasons, it may be a good idea to include any file number or other reference on this line.

People who use a reference or subject line have a wide range of ideas about whether to locate it to the left or at the centre of the page, and how it should be written. Some use bold print, italics, all capital letters, underlining and any combination of these, with further ideas about spacing. One feature of the reference or subject line is its variety. Even the exact meaning of the expression 'Re' is controversial, although it probably originated in the legal texts of the common law where it means 'In the matter of' the particular case under discussion. 'Re' is almost certainly not short for 'Reference line' or the expression 'In relation to'.

Body

The most important aspect of letter writing is what you say in the body or middle part of your letter. But looks are also important and, given the large number of competing and eye-catching demands for the attention of the person you are writing to, it is worthwhile making your letter visually balanced and appealing. Make an effort to space the paragraphs evenly and limit the number of points you are making, as in Letter 2.6 to the boss of BHP Limited. This letter involves the same parcel of land where the rifle range and shooting complex was proposed, as described in Letter 1.1.

2.6   Complaint letter

Mr Paul Anderson
Chief Executive Officer
BHP Limited
GPO Box 86A
MELBOURNE VIC 3001

Dear Mr Anderson,

I have been working on a private member's bill to declare the Dharawal State Recreation Area near Wollongong and Campbell-town a national park down to a depth of 100 metres. This will protect the surface ecosystems, including plant and animal habitats, and at the same time allow the BHP longwall coal mining program in the Illawarra region to continue. I understand mining takes place at 500 metres below the surface.

One matter that does concern me is the effect of mine subsidence on the Dharawal's upland swamps, which represent some of the most significant ecosystems of their type in the world. As you would know, mine subsidence has caused the Georges River to crack with the consequent loss of a significant volume of water. Similar loss of water from the upland swamps would be an environmental disaster of catastrophic proportions.

I would be obliged if you could inform me by return letter of your plans to mine under the Dharawal and what safeguards you intend to put in place to protect the upland swamps. The value of these swamps cannot be overstated and currently they are the subject of an application for World Heritage listing with the Commonwealth Government. A brochure about the swamps is attached.

You may be aware that an application to extend clay mining leases adjoining the Dharawal is opposed by local councils and environ-mental groups. The case will be heard in the Land and Environment Court in the near future and I am confident the court will put an end to the clay mining, which is highly destructive of one section of the upland swamps.

Needless to say, it will be a pyrrhic victory if the clay mining is halted and still longwall coal mining drains all the water from the swamps. My advice to the local councils and environmental groups is to commence an action in public nuisance against BHP if the necessary assurances about protecting the Dharawal from mine subsidence are not forthcoming.

I look forward to your urgent reply.

Yours sincerely,

P. Breen

Peter Breen

Each paragraph in this letter is more or less the same length and the points made in the first paragraph are carried through to the end in a story. Perhaps only the second last paragraph contains a new idea, and then only for the purpose of giving notice of the possibility of legal action. Importantly, the letter seeks to reduce a complex story (a nightmare, to be exact) to a simple narrative involving the conflict between coal mining and the environment. The letter brought instant action, by the way, and BHP called a meeting of all the interest groups to address our concerns.

Before leaving the body of your letter, it is worth noting that letters have different formats including full-block, semi-block and simplified or abbreviated. Nothing much turns on these formats except the fact that your letter needs to be consistent if you want it to look good. With full-block letters all lines are flush with the left margin. For semi-block letters the reference line, complimentary close and signature line are moved to the centre of the page, and the date appears flush with the right margin.

The abbreviated or simplified letter is more like a memo and will be discussed further in Chapter Three in the context of email letters.

Complimentary close

The complimentary close is conventionally linked directly to the salutation so these are not difficult choices to make. Like the salutation the complimentary close is important because it sets the tone in your letter. If you say 'Dear Mr Smith' in the salutation, this is a formal address which should be followed by the formal complimentary close 'Yours faithfully'. On the other hand, if you use the informal salutation 'Dear John', this should be followed by the informal complimentary close 'Yours sincerely'. The WriteQuick letter writing system lists various options available in two groups, one formal and the other informal.

Formal salutation and complimentary close

Salutation	Complimentary close
• Dear (title and surname)	• Very truly yours
• Dear Sir	• Sincerely
• Dear Madam	• Very sincerely
• Dear Colleague	• Yours faithfully
• Dear Executive	• Yours sincerely
• Dear Secretary	• With kind regards

In the United Kingdom and Australia, the most popular formal complimentary close is 'Yours faithfully', although 'Yours sincerely' is also popular, and I must say it is my preference. If you receive a formal letter from the United States it will include the complimentary close 'Very truly yours' or perhaps 'Sincerely'. The Americans also like variations on these two expressions including 'Very sincerely', 'Yours truly', 'Truly yours' and 'Sincerely yours'. The WriteQuick program also lists various informal salutation and complimentary close options.

Informal salutation and complimentary close

Salutation	Complimentary close
• Dear (first name)	• Yours truly
• My dear (first name)	• Sincerely
• Hello	• Yours sincerely
• Dear friend	• With fond regards
• My dear friend	• With best wishes
• Good morning	• Affectionately yours

Common usage in the United Kingdom and Australia is 'Yours sincerely' for the informal complimentary close. As always, the situation in the United States is not so straightforward with 'Yours truly', 'Sincerely' (again, with its several variations) and 'Best regards' and 'Best wishes' all vying for attention. When in doubt about the appropriate complimentary close, stick to an option consistent with the salutation and popular use. In fact, you can try any number of options using the WriteQuick program provided you keep separate the formal and informal options.

One final word about the complimentary close and salutation relates to punctuation. Personally, I like to see a comma after both as it signifies a pause, which is appropriate following a greeting to your correspondent. I believe the greeting loses something if you launch straight into the body of the letter following the salutation. Similarly, the complimentary close is diminished if you appear to be rushing to conclude your letter. It is a personal matter, however, and I recognise that the Write-Quick program does not include punctuation for the reasons of convenience already mentioned.

Signature

The signature block (the complimentary close and your name) will be flush against the left margin in a full-block letter or in the centre of the page in a semi-block letter. You should type your name under your signature to avoid the embarrassment that your correspondent may not recognise who you are from your autograph. Sign off with your first name only if you are writing to a friend. If you do not know the person you are writing to, and it is not clear from your name whether you are a man or a woman, add the title 'Mr' or 'Ms' after your name in parentheses.

Yours faithfully,

Leigh Adams (Ms)

Yours sincerely,

Lyn Kingma (Mr)

Some people will be recognised by their job title and it is usually inserted immediately below their printed name. In such a case, hopefully, it will not be necessary to identify a person's gender.

Yours faithfully,

Kim Beazley
Member for Brand

Yours sincerely,

Laurie Brereton
Member for Kingsford Smith

If you are signing on behalf of somebody else, simply sign 'Per' followed by your own signature. Alternatively, sign the person's name with some identification mark such as your initials to indicate you have signed for the person. Some people just sign 'For John Smith' and leave it to the reader to work out who might have signed the letter. When you sign on behalf of a company or other organisation, include your position under your printed name, and the name of the company or organisation immediately below the complimentary close.

Yours sincerely,
Heart to Heart Communications

Olwyn Dearheart

Olwyn Dearheart (Ms)
Chief Executive Officer

Yours sincerely,
Pleasant Park Darts Club

Johnny Walker

Johnny Walker
President

You may have noticed on correspondence from law and accountancy partnerships that the firm name will often appear below the complimentary close, as in other letters from companies and organisations, but the letter has no designated signatory. The author of the letter will simply sign the letter in the name of the firm in the mistaken belief that they are not individually responsible for the contents of the letter. A variation on this practice is to simply print the name of the firm under the complimentary close and 'sign' the name of the firm, again, so as not to identify the author.

Yours faithfully,
Budgie & Parrot

Budgie + Parrot

Yours faithfully,

Budgie + Parrot

Simply signing the firm name is a doubtful practice in the sense that you are responsible for what you say in a letter, whether or not you sign it. If you make a mistake you can always correct the record, with another letter, and if you are disinclined to follow that course, your aggrieved correspondent might wish to seek consolation in the defamation laws. In making amends for an error in a letter, however, always seek advice as your attempts at reconciliation could amount to an admission of liability for the consequences of your letter (see Chapter Four).

Postscript and enclosures

After the signature line you might want to add a postscript to your letter, adding further information as an afterthought, or perhaps repeating some point made earlier in the letter for emphasis. Sales letters in particular will often make an offer or give a guarantee in the postscript. It seems that many people read the postscript at the foot of the sales letter before they read anything else. Companies like Reader's Digest and Encyclopaedia Britannica have created multimillion dollar enterprises on the back of the humble postscript.

The end of the letter is also a good place to refer to enclosures. It is a useful reminder when despatching the letter that you need to add additional information to the envelope. Adding the word 'encl.' or its plural form 'encls.' also alerts your correspondent to the fact that your letter refers to extraneous material that ought to be attached. If you write a large number of letters, adopting this practice will allow you to see at a glance whether your mailing package is ready for despatch when you sign it.

Another useful addition at the end of your correspondence is the letters 'cc.' (meaning 'carbon copy') followed by the name of the person or persons you are sending a copy of the letter. You need to be careful about privacy and confidentiality (not to mention defamation) when you are sending a copy of your letter to a person other than your correspondent. If you are writing the letter as a professional on behalf of a client you need to be doubly careful about copies of the letter. In such a case you would send a copy of your letter to another person only with the express permission of your client.

Forms of address

Here we will consider the many ways to address a person in a letter. Everybody has a title one way or another, and rather than put off writing a letter because you are uncertain how to address a person, simply look up their title in one of the following lists. The lists allow you to choose between the formal and informal forms of address for most public and private officials. Unfortunately, the lists are not exhaustive and do not include members of the armed forces or police officers, for example. As I said earlier, do not use the informal form of address unless you know the person. If you wonder whether the person remembers you, err on the side of caution and use the formal form of address.

Some members of parliament have complimentary or courtesy titles which you might want to use in your correspondence. Upper House members of State parliaments and federal and State government ministers may be addressed in a letter as 'The Honourable' or 'The Hon.'. These titles are optional, representing a legacy from days when ministers and Upper House members of parliament received no remuneration for their services to the community. The President of the New South Wales Legislative Council, Dr Meredith Burgmann, has ruled that nothing in the parliament's standing orders requires that members refer to each other as 'The Honourable'. Presumably the same ruling applies to correspondence. Judges also enjoy the complimentary title 'The Honourable' or 'The Hon.' and again, many people believe the honorific to be an anachronism. I use complimentary titles in the following examples but you will not be alone if you omit them in your letters.

Women and men

Most women these days rightly insist on being treated equally to men. For this reason the title 'Mrs', which nominates the marital status of a woman, has fallen out of favour and been replaced with the title 'Ms' which says nothing about a woman's marital status. If a woman prefers to be addressed as 'Mrs' in a letter, however, it would be wrong not to respect her wishes. Even the titles 'Miss' and 'Master' for young people may be replaced with 'Ms' and 'Mr' as the case may be. For men, the title 'Mr' is uncomplicated so far as their marital status is concerned. The title 'Esquire' or 'Esq.' after a man's name was never common in Australia. The French titles 'Madam' and 'Monsieur' (and their many variations) are rarely used. Married couples and people living together require special forms of address, as do same-sex couples and people sharing the same household. The following list of popular forms of address and relevant salutations may be useful.

Form of address	Salutation	
	Formal	Informal
Ms Mary Jones	Dear Ms Jones,	Dear Mary,
Mrs Anna Brown	Dear Mrs Brown,	Dear Anna,
Ms Mary Jones & Mrs Anna Brown	Dear Ms Jones & Mrs Brown,	Dear Mary & Anna,
Ms Trish Wong & Ms Zoe Chan	Dear Ms Wong & Ms Chan,	Dear Trish & Zoe,
Mr John Smith	Dear Mr Smith,	Dear John,
Mr John Smith & Mr Bill Black	Dear Mr Smith & Mr Black,	Dear John & Bill,
Ms Mary Jones & Mr John Smith	Dear Ms Jones & Mr Smith,	Dear Mary & John,
Mrs Anna Brown & Mr John Smith	Dear Mrs. Brown & Mr Smith,	Dear Anna & John,
Mrs Lucy Smith & Mr John Smith	Dear Mrs & Mr Smith,	Dear Lucy & John,
Mr John Smith & Mrs Lucy Smith	Dear Mr & Mrs Smith,	Dear John & Lucy,

Company office bearers

The head of a corporation in Australia is usually called the 'Chief Executive Officer' or the 'Managing Director'. In other countries such as the United States, the 'President' or sometimes the 'Chairman of the Board' will be responsible for the day to day running of a corporation. Addressing corporate executives by reference to their position in the company is not so common in Australia. For the female executive, one battle that seems to have no end is her correct title and form of address. Political correctness would suggest that the 'Chair of the Board' would be more appropriate than Chairman but as one woman boss of a large corporation told me, she thinks of the term 'chair' as the furniture you sit on. Some women and men prefer 'Chairperson' although the word does lack a certain ring. It is an argument I am reluctant to buy into when so many women prefer using the title 'Chairman'. Subject to that caveat I can offer the following suggested forms of address and salutation for corporate executives.

| Form of address | Salutation | |
	Formal	Informal
Ms Anna Brown Chairman	Dear Madam Chairman, or Dear Ms Brown,	Dear Anna, or Dear Ms Brown,
Mr John Smith President	Dear Mr President, or Dear Mr Smith,	Dear John, or Dear Mr Smith,
Ms Mary Jones Vice President	Dear Madam Vice President, or Dear Ms Jones,	Dear Mary, or Dear Ms Jones,
Mr Bill Black Secretary	Dear Mr Secretary, or Dear Mr. Black,	Dear Bill, or Dear Mr Black,
Ms Doris Park Treasurer	Dear Madam Treasurer, or Dear Ms Park,	Dear Doris, or Dear Ms Park,

Local government

Sometimes described as the third tier of government, local government is where many of us interface with the democratic process. Local government is true grassroots democracy and most of the letters we write to government officials will be addressed to the local council. For all that, local government only exists at the pleasure of the State government, and if you have a serious problem with your local council, you may need to write to the minister for local government in the State government. Normally, complaints about the local council will be investigated by the ombudsman. When writing to the council, only elected officials have formal titles so do not make the mistake in your letter of addressing the town planner, health inspector or environmental liaison officer by any title other than 'Mr' or 'Ms' as the case may be. The following forms of address and salutation may be useful when writing to your elected members of the local council.

| Form of address | Salutation | |
	Formal	Informal
Mr Tom Wilson Mayor	Dear Mayor Wilson, or Dear Mr Wilson,	Dear Tom, or Dear Mr Wilson,
Ms May West Deputy Mayor	Dear Deputy Mayor West, or Dear Ms West,	Dear May, or Dear Ms West,
Ms Vicki Woods Shire President	Dear Shire President Woods, or Dear Ms Woods,	Dear Vicki, or Dear Ms Woods,
Mr Bill East Deputy Shire President	Dear Deputy Shire President East, or Dear Mr East,	Dear Bill, or Dear Mr East,
Ms Verlie Fowler Councillor	Dear Councillor Fowler, or Dear Ms Fowler,	Dear Verlie, or Dear Ms Fowler

State government

The notional head of the State of New South Wales is the governor, Professor Marie Bashir AO. Although her husband is a knight, Sir Nicholas Shehadie, the governor chooses not to use the complimentary title 'Lady' or the honorific 'The Honourable'. Responsibility for running the State rests with the premier who enjoys the support of a majority of members of the Legislative Assembly. Members of the Legislative Council review legislation and represent community interests in parliament. Heads of government departments and public authorities may have formal titles attaching to their position, but you would not normally address them by their titles in a letter. Here is a list of forms of

address and salutation that cover formal titles in the State
government.

Form of address	Salutation	
	Formal	Informal
Her Excellency Professor Marie Bashir AO Governor of New South Wales	Your Excellency, or Dear Governor,	Dear Professor Bashir, or Dear Governor,
The Hon. Robert Carr MP Premier	Dear Premier, or Dear Mr Carr,	Dear Bob, or Dear Mr Carr,
The Hon. Dr Andrew Refshauge MP Deputy Premier	Dear Deputy Premier, or Dear Dr Refshauge,	Dear Andrew, or Dear Dr Refshauge,
The Hon. Michael Egan MLC Treasurer	Dear Treasurer, or Dear Mr Egan,	Dear Michael, or Dear Mr Egan,
The Hon. Carl Scully MP Minister for Roads	Dear Minister, or Dear Mr Scully,	Dear Carl, or Dear Mr Scully,
Mr Graham West MP Legislative Assembly	Dear Mr West,	Dear Graham, or Dear Mr West,
The Hon. Dr Peter Wong MLC Legislative Council	Dear Dr Wong,	Dear Peter, or Dear Dr Wong,

Commonwealth government

Australia's head of state is Queen Elizabeth II who resides in
England. Her royal coat of arms can be seen on many public
buildings, even buildings constructed in the last few years. The
Queen's representative in Australia is the governor-general. Below
the governor-general in our democratic hierarchy is the prime
minister who does not rate a mention in the Australian
Constitution (though the queen is mentioned 43 times). After
the prime minister are the other ministers, followed by members
of the House of Representatives and the Senate. As in the State
parliaments, heads of government departments and public
authorities would not normally be addressed in a letter by their

formal titles. The following forms of address and salutation may be used in a letter to the Commonwealth government.

Form of address	Salutation	
	Formal	Informal
Her Majesty Queen Elizabeth II Queen of Australia	Your Majesty,	Dear Queen Elizabeth II,
His Excellency The Right Rev. Dr Peter Hollingworth AC, OBE	Your Excellency, or Dear Governor-General,	Dear Dr Hollingworth, or Dear Governor-General,
The Hon. John Howard MP Prime Minister	Dear Prime Minister, or Dear Mr Howard,	Dear John, or Dear Mr Howard,
The Hon. John Anderson MP Deputy Prime Minister	Dear Deputy Prime Minister, Dear Mr Anderson,	Dear John, or Dear Mr Anderson,
The Hon. Alexander Downer MP Minister for Foreign Affairs	Dear Minister, or Dear Mr Downer,	Dear Alexander, or Dear Mr Downer,
The Hon. Larry Anthony MP Minister for Community Services	Dear Minister, or Dear Mr Anthony,	Dear Larry, or Dear Mr Anthony,
Mrs Trish Draper MP House of Representatives	Dear Member, or Dear Mrs Draper,	Dear Trish, or Dear Mrs Draper,
Senator The Hon. Dr Bob Brown The Senate	Dear Senator Brown, or Dear Dr Brown	Dear Bob, or Dear Dr Brown,

Court officials

Judges too are part of the government, but distinct from the politicians under the Westminster parliament's separation of powers doctrine. The authority of judges in Australia is derived from Chapter Three of the Australian Constitution. Courts operate on a hierarchy beginning with the Local Court, District or County Court, State Supreme Court, Federal Court and the High Court. Except for the Local Court, each court has an appeals jurisdiction. A number of appeals boards and tribunals also have judicial functions and their officers may be judges, commissioners or members. Usually you would include the formal

title of any judicial officer in a letter. Here is a list of the forms
of address and salutation for selected judicial officers.

| Form of address | Salutation | |
	Formal	Informal
The Hon. Justice Mary Gaudron High Court	Your Honour, or Dear Justice Gaudron,	Dear Judge, or Dear Justice Gaudron,
The Hon. Justice Murray Wilcox Federal Court	Your Honour, or Dear Justice Wilcox,	Dear Judge, or Dear Justice Wilcox,
The Hon. Justice Greg James Supreme Court	Your Honour, or Dear Justice James,	Dear Judge, or Dear Justice James,
The Hon. Leone Glynn Industrial Court	Your Honour, or Dear Judge Glynn,	Dear Judge, or Dear Judge Glynn,
The Hon. Mahla Pearlman AM Land and Environment Court	Your Honour, or Dear Judge Pearlman,	Dear Judge, or Dear Judge Pearlman,
The Hon. Justice Michael Campbell Compensation Court	Your Honour, or Dear Justice Campbell,	Dear Judge, or Dear Justice Campbell,
His Honour Judge Bob Bellear District Court	Your Honour, or Dear Judge Bellear,	Dear Judge, or Dear Judge Bellear,
His Honour Judge Kevin O'Connor Fair Trading Tribunal	Your Honour, or Dear Judge O'Connor,	Dear Judge, or Dear Judge O'Connor,
Ms Patricia Staunton Chief Magistrate	Your Worship, or Dear Ms Staunton,	Dear Patricia, or Dear Ms Staunton,

Diplomatic officials

Australia has foreign representatives in most countries of the
world. As well as diplomatic and trade officials, the Department
of Foreign Affairs employs support staff in various key positions.
All diplomatic officials have formal titles and, like court officials,
you would generally include their formal title in a letter.
Consular and trade officials who have an active role to play in
promoting Australia's interests overseas are also regarded as
diplomatic officials. Foreign representatives in ascending hierarchy are consul general, high commissioner and ambassador.

Here is a list of diplomatic officials and their formal titles as you would address them in a letter, along with the relevant salutations.

| | Salutation | |
Form of address	Formal	Informal
Ms Penny Wensley, Ambassador to the United Nations	Your Excellency, or Dear Ambassador,	Dear Penny, or Dear Ms Wensley,
Mr Ross Burns Ambassador to Greece	Your Excellency, or Dear Ambassador,	Dear Ross, or Dear Mr Burns,
Mr Michael L'Estrange, High Commissioner to London	Your Excellency, or Dear High Commissioner,	Dear Michael, or Dear Mr L'Estrange,
Mr Ken Allen, Consul-General in New York	Dear Consul-General, or Dear Mr Allen,	Dear Ken, or Dear Mr Allen,

Academics and professionals

Medical practitioners, veterinarians and dentists all use the complimentary title 'Dr' as do chiropractors and osteopaths in all States and Territories except New South Wales. A doctor may have an academic or professional degree. Either way, the complimentary title 'Dr' replaces 'Mr' or 'Mrs' as the case may be. Where the person has another title, this title precedes the academic or professional title. The President of the New South Wales Legislative Council, for example, is addressed in a letter as 'The Hon. Dr Meredith Burgmann MLC'. A letter to the new governor-general of Australia will be addressed 'His Excellency The Right Rev. Dr Peter Hollingworth AC, OBE'.

Some people argue that the only real doctors are those who deliver babies, but real doctors in my book hold doctorates conferred by recognised tertiary institutions including theological colleges. Like government officials and company office bearers, academics have a hierarchy. The ascending hierarchy for academics is lecturer, senior lecturer, associate professor, professor, dean, pro vice-chancellor, deputy vice-chancellor and vice-chancellor. The chancellor is not usually an academic. Following is a list of selected academics and their formal titles as you would address them in a letter, together with the appropriate salutations.

Form of address	Salutation	
	Formal	Informal
Professor Roger Holmes Vice-Chancellor University of Newcastle	Dear Vice-Chancellor, or Dear Professor Holmes,	Dear Roger, or Dear Professor Holmes,
Professor Brian English Deputy Vice-Chancellor University of Newcastle	Dear Deputy Vice-Chancellor, or Dear Professor English,	Dear Brian, or Dear Professor English,
Professor Jenny Graham Pro Vice-Chancellor University of Newcastle	Dear Pro Vice-Chancellor, or Dear Professor Graham,	Dear Jenny, or Dear Professor Graham,
Professor Anne Finlay Dean, Faculty of Law University of Newcastle	Dear Dean, or Dear Professor Finlay,	Dear Anne, or Dear Professor Finlay,
Mrs Jo Cooper Senior Lecturer, Faculty of Law University of Newcastle	Dear Mrs Cooper,	Dear Jo, or Dear Mrs Cooper,

Religious leaders

Jewish and Christian faiths share their origins in the Hebrew sacred texts and one consequence of this common ancestry is the prominence of religious clergy. Some differences occur in the form of address between Protestant and Roman Catholic Churches. In other religions such as Islam (which also shares the origins of the Jewish and Christian faiths), Hinduism and Buddhism, religious scholars are the spiritual leaders who serve their respective communities, and each scholar has a particular form of address. In Islam, religious teachers and scholars are sometimes given the complimentary title 'mullah' while the head of a mosque is known as 'imam'. Here is a list of forms of address and salutation as they apply to selected religious leaders.

Form of address	Salutation	
	Formal	Informal
His Holiness Pope John Paul II Bishop of Rome	Your Holiness,	Most Holy Father,
His Eminence Cardinal Edward Clancy Emeritus Archbishop of Sydney	Your Eminence, or Dear Cardinal Clancy,	Dear Cardinal Clancy,
The Most Rev. Peter Watson Archbishop of Melbourne	Your Grace, or Dear Archbishop Watson,	Dear Archbishop Watson,
The Most Rev. Philip Wilson Coadjutor Archbishop of Adelaide	Your Grace, or Dear Archbishop Wilson,	Dear Archbishop Wilson,
The Right Rev. Louise Carter Bishop of Women's Ministry	Reverend Bishop, or Dear Bishop Carter,	Dear Bishop Louise, or Dear Bishop Carter,
Rev. Monsignor Alf White Diocese of Lismore	Reverend Monsignor, or Dear Monsignor White,	Dear Monsignor Alf, or Dear Monsignor White,
Rev. Father Paul Jones Bangalow Presbytery	Reverend Father, or Dear Father Jones,	Dear Father Paul, or Dear Father Jones,
Rev. Carol Jones Abbotsford Rectory.	Reverend Jones, or Dear Reverend Jones,	Dear Reverend Carol, or Dear Reverend Jones,
Sister Mary McCarthy Ascension Convent	Reverend Sister, or Dear Sister McCarthy,	Dear Sister Mary, or Dear Sister McCarthy,
Brother Pat O'Flynn Marist Mission	Reverend Brother, or Dear Brother O'Flynn,	Dear Brother Pat, or Dear Brother O'Flynn,
Rabbi Frank Cohen Great Synagogue	Rabbi, or Dear Rabbi Cohen,	Dear Rabbi, or Dear Rabbi Cohen,
Imam Ali Aklar Hussein Sultan Ahmet Mosque	Assalam Aliakom, or Dear Imam Hussein,	Dear Imam, or Dear Imam Hussein,
Mullah El Habib Al Saisal College	Assalam Aliakom, or Dear Mullah Habib	Dear Mullah, or Dear Mullah Habib,
Guru Ram Chandra Satyananda Ashram	Guru, or Dear Guru Chandra,	Dear Guru, or Dear Guru Chandra,

The next chapter deals with strategies for producing effective letters, including the actual writing of the letter. Your correspondence will be most effective when the body of the letter literally jumps off the page at your reader. We also look at language and how to develop techniques for avoiding common mistakes in grammar and style. Finally, we ask the perennial letter writer's question—post, fax or email?

Chapter Three

Strategies

How to begin

At this point we might return to the first letter at the beginning of the book, Letter 1.1 to Premier Robert Carr about the shooting complex. You will recall the four key features you need to identify before writing an effective letter: the person you intend writing to, the issue you want to address in your letter, the purpose of your letter or the link between the person you are writing to and the issue, and the action you want the person to take.

Once you have identified the four key features—and two or three points you intend making in the letter—you are ready to begin writing. Some people like to talk the issue through with a friend or colleague while others rely on a burst of creative energy to get their ideas onto paper. For me, brainstorming what I want to say in a few short sentences is an effective technique for getting started.

Brainstorming

Bearing in mind the four key features of your letter, start writing the first thing that comes to mind about the person you are writing to. Why that person and not somebody else? How can that person help you solve your problem? Has the person said something about the problem? Recently I had a problem with the Commonwealth Bank. In fact, it was a longstanding grievance brought to mind by two incidents that occurred last Boxing Day. Previously I had decided I could do nothing about the problem except wait for the passage of time, but the two incidents spurred me on to give the bank a blast, even though no action came to mind as a solution to the problem. I worked myself into a frenzy and began brainstorming.

> A pox on the Commonwealth Bank. Write to the boss and give him a blast. Draw his attention to the article in the *Herald* about bank charges. What an outrage for the poxy bank to destroy a child's bank account with bank charges. Did the bank's boss know the child was saving to buy Christmas presents? Tell him the poxy bank logo on the sightboard ruined the Boxing Day Test. The bank represents corporate greed, but cricket belongs to the people. Somehow link cricket with the need for a charges-free account for the poor. Have a good whinge about the bank's credit reporting policy. I paid the lousy $1900, albeit late. None of my other creditors reported me as a bad credit risk. Must carry large amounts of cash when I travel because I cannot get a credit card. A pox on credit cards and those who require them as security. A person without a credit card is presumed to be a crook. Remember 1911 when the Commonwealth Bank was the people's bank. Finish with another blast about the poxy credit reporting policy.

Brainstorming the salient points I wanted to make in a few short sentences allowed the inconvenience of not having a credit card to emerge as an issue. Presumably the boss of the Commonwealth Bank spends a good deal of time travelling and he would be aware in some general way of the stigma attached to a regular traveller with no credit card. Well, perhaps. In any event, I had at least one theme for the letter, and a suitable tone was emerging.

It is worth noting that no action statement came to mind for the end of this letter. But I had the beginning of the letter and two or three points I wanted to make. Because I knew nothing about the boss of the bank, I rang the bank for his name and more information. Though I tried not to sound like a serial killer, needless to say the bank would tell me nothing. So, I had no way to link the bank boss to my problem. Nevertheless, I did have the benefit of an active imagination. Letter 3.1 is the full text of the final version of the letter to the bank.

3.1 Bank complaint letter

Mr David Murray   26 December 2000
Managing Director
Commonwealth Bank
GPO Box 2719
SYDNEY NSW 1155

Dear Mr Murray,

Two things happened today, prompting me to write to you.

I read in Column 8 of the *Sydney Morning Herald* that you deducted $3.40 in bank charges from the account of a small child, thereby placing the account in debit. Then you charged the account with a $25 overdrawn account fee. The child had been saving to buy Christmas presents.

Later I sat down to watch the Boxing Day Cricket Test on television. At the end of the Melbourne Cricket Ground, adorning the sightboard, I was appalled to see your black and yellow corporate logo. You put me right off the game with the caption 'Make it happen' under the logo. Already much has happened at your instigation.

Just to place you in the picture, a few years ago I fell on hard times, including several months of unemployment. My creditors included your Commonwealth Bank to whom I was indebted for the sum of $1900. Although I paid the amount in full, the payment was late, and as a result you gave me an adverse credit rating.

I cannot begin to tell you the trouble the adverse credit rating has caused. Even now, despite my changed circumstances, I am unable for example to obtain a credit card. Whenever I travel I am obliged to carry sufficient cash to pay hotel and car hire expenses. Vast amounts of cash are required as security deposits because it is presumed that a person without a credit card is a crook.

You were my smallest creditor when times were tough and yet you have caused me the most trouble. Nobody else saw fit to impugn my good name and reputation by reporting me as a bad credit risk. It is simply not true. I have always paid my bills and usually on time. These days I pay early.

You have come a long way since 1911 when the federal Labor government established your bank 'to represent the people's needs rather than the profit motive'. Personally, I have no objection to the profit motive although it is rather obscene that Australia's most profitable corporations are banks. What we need is another people's bank—the kind of bank you were in 1911.

In a consumer-oriented society like the one we enjoy in Australia you are more or less free to operate in whatever way you please. But it is extremely galling to see your hard and uncaring corporate face on a nice game like cricket, as if usury were somehow a respectable activity. You will never be respectable until you introduce a charges-free account for the disadvantaged and the poor.

On the question of my adverse credit rating, the passage of time will no doubt solve my problems. I am amazed, however, that the banking industry uses negative credit reporting without at the same time employing the services of positive credit agencies.

Yours sincerely,

Peter Breen

Developing ideas

I imagined the boss of the Commonwealth Bank as a nice man who began his career as a bank teller. He was deeply saddened that automatic teller machines now performed the same tasks he once carried out so diligently. Somehow they made his work in the early years look meaningless and repetitive. These insidious wall monsters had nearly cost him his employment and he was sympathetic to the circumstances in which a fellow traveller (in the 'big picture' sense) found himself on the dole. In the light of this conjecture, of course, I needed to moderate the language that emerged in my brainstorming. If I wanted to be taken seriously with my missive I needed to strike a heart chord with the bank boss, and I would not do that by being offensive.

I was assisted in my efforts to appeal to the bank manager's heart by the newspaper article about the child's bank account. The bank had knocked the account for six with bank charges (though I decided against this metaphor as I explain later) when the child was saving to buy Christmas presents. Also, the Commonwealth Bank was formerly the people's bank, set up by a Labor government in 1911. It was possible to link this theme in the letter, as well as the idea that cricket belongs to the people. Finding the right theme led to a suitable tone. It needed to be polite but firm. The bank's logo 'Make it happen' was provocative and I needed to modify my instinctive reaction to send a rocket letter, otherwise I had no chance of receiving a reply.

Consumer pressure on banks to lift their service game and distribute their massive profits more equitably is relentless. In the last six months the Commonwealth Bank made $1.1 billion profit. When the profit was announced, the bank informed customers that fees of up to $75 would be charged on some transactions. At this rate, having a bank account in Australia may soon be a status symbol. A recent decision by United Kingdom banks, on the other hand, means no fees are charged in that country on automatic teller machine transactions. In Europe, positive credit reporting is no less important than the negative reporting I had experienced in Australia, and this was another theme I could develop. I risked making the letter too complicated, however, and at that point I needed to begin writing. Once you write down your ideas in sequence they appear less complex, and your letter will soon take shape.

The process of drafting

Begin by writing down in one sentence the incident or incidents that prompted you to write the letter. If one sentence is unwieldy, simply begin by saying, 'Two things happened today, prompting me to write to you.' Perhaps you are writing about only one incident, in which case you could begin your letter with, 'Something happened today, prompting me to write to you.' The sentence may not be earth shattering, but you have begun. If you are writing about more than one incident, avoid describing them as 'Firstly', 'Secondly', 'Thirdly' and so on. You are passing a death sentence on your letter if you write like that. Only judges use that kind of language and it is one reason their judgments are unreadable.

Referring back to the present example, two incidents prompted the letter, one being the newspaper report of the child's bank account, and the other the appearance of the bank's advertising as an unwelcome guest at the cricket. Each incident can be described in separate paragraphs comprising two or three sentences. It is a mistake to think you can run the incidents together or describe them in the same metaphorical language. Although I was sorely tempted to tell the bank boss he had hit the child's bank account for six, using this metaphor would have meant confusing two completely unrelated incidents.

Your opening paragraphs need to be personal—that is, directed to the person you are writing to. Use the pronouns 'you' and 'your' to tie the person to the incident or incidents you are writing about. When I wrote to the bank boss, I held him personally responsible for the interest on the child's bank account as well as the advertising at the cricket, even though he probably wasn't directly responsible for either incident. One good reason for writing to the boss of an organisation is the person at the top is ultimately responsible for everything. Also, a letter to the boss almost certainly guarantees a response.

By the second or third paragraph of your letter you ought to be focusing on the issue you are writing about. In the present example I did not get to my credit card grievance until the fourth paragraph, which means the letter is a bit long winded. I justified the extra words on the basis that the letter was just a whinge—I had no action in mind that the bank might take to restore my adverse credit rating. The difficulty with credit agencies is they represent a law unto themselves, and once they give you a black mark, you keep it for five years. No amount of solicitation by the bank or anybody else would change the record—the account was paid late and I was a reprobate.

You may be lucky enough to write down what you want to say and get it right the first time. If this is the case, pat yourself on the back because generally you need to write and rewrite before the right words emerge. My own technique for drafting a letter is to focus on the main point I want to make (in the present example my inability to get a credit card), locate the point somewhere in the middle of the letter, build up to it in the beginning and fade away at the end. If the opportunity arises I may repeat the point as I close the letter, or perhaps express it in some other way as a postscript. Try and focus on the process of drafting rather than the outcome. If you get the process right your letter will develop a life of its own.

The body

The body is literally the guts of your letter where you press home the issue to your correspondent in such a way that you hope they feel personally responsible for your problem. While you are explaining and expanding on the issue, you will also be emphasising the purpose of your letter—the personal link between the issue and the person you are writing to. The process may take one or two paragraphs, depending upon how many points you are trying to make. Link the paragraphs as best you can without confusing your ideas. What you are looking for is continuity in your letter and the secret is 'transitions', which are words, phrases or sentences that take your reader from one idea to the next.

Transition words and phrases

Reviewing the letter to the boss of the bank, several ideas were important, and it was necessary to list them in a logical sequence. Because my problem arose several years before the particular incidents I was writing about, I needed to use a transition phrase to bridge the time gap. I began the third paragraph with the phrase 'Just to the place you in the picture'. Similarly, when I wanted to refer back to the bank's origins, I began paragraph six with the transition phrase 'You have come a long way since 1911'. Time words such as 'then', 'when', and 'later' achieve the same purpose. In paragraph four, where I get to the heart of the problem, I attempted to link the adverse credit rating of several years ago to my current predicament of not having a credit card by using the transition words 'Even now'. The following transition words and phrases may assist you to link your ideas.

Time: then; when; later; next; meanwhile; previously; afterwards; now; later; earlier; often; some time; another time; formerly; even now; etc.

Space: away from; next to; beyond; between; around; over; above; below; inside; outside; etc.

Additional point:	furthermore; moreover; in addition; also; besides; finally; added to that; for example; for instance; etc.
Cause and effect:	thereby; consequently; as a result; thus; therefore; etc.
Similarity:	similarly; in the same vein; likewise; like; as with; etc.
Difference:	by way of contrast; on the other hand; instead of; although; nevertheless; but; regrettably; unfortunately; etc.
Emphasis:	the point is; as you know; in fact; most important; more importantly; indeed; above all; in other words; etc.
Concession:	granted; that said; of course; yet; in any event; after all; needless to say; etc.
Conclusion:	and therefore; summing up; in conclusion; as a result; to sum up; in brief; in conclusion; finally; at last; etc.

Repeating key words and phrases

In my letter to the bank boss, the phrase 'adverse credit rating' appears three times, including in the last paragraph for emphasis. Somebody reading your letter (who may or may not be the person you are writing to) will make an instant decision either to address your problem or put your letter to one side. The person needs to know your problem—and they will get your message only if you repeat it several times. If you are concerned about driving your reader to distraction, use synonyms (different words with the same meaning) or similar phrases to make the same point. Even contrasting phrases can be useful. In the final paragraph of my letter to the bank boss, I actually made the same point three times using different phrases.

On the question of my _adverse credit rating_, the passage of time will no doubt solve my problems. I am amazed, however, that the banking industry uses _negative credit reporting_ without at the same time employing the services of _positive credit agencies_.

Another useful repetition device is to repeat the pronouns 'you' and 'your'. This is one sure way to hold your reader's attention even at the risk of driving him or her mad. Again, referring to the letter to the bank boss, after the salutation 'Dear Mr Murray', I actually used the words 'you' or 'your' nineteen times. You may think this is a bit over the top, but neither word appears in the critical last paragraph of the letter since I decided not to end on a personal note. Do not fear repetition in your letters so long as you also use contrasting styles and vary your expression to avoid losing the attention of your reader.

Some letters are so repetitive in their style and expression they literally beat your reader over the head, which is not conducive to receiving a meaningful response. You need to vary your sentence structure and style in the same way you pause, use body language and raise or lower your voice when you speak. Of course, if you speak in a monotone you may write in a rut. Try singing when you write to make your words dance off the page. Say something that goes _clunk_ if you want to change your style. A word like 'crook' can do it, and I used this word in the middle of the letter to the bank boss. (However, notice I did not specifically identify any particular person as a crook.)

Linking paragraphs

One big problem with using 'clunk' words is that you may not be able to use them to link ideas, and they are especially a problem at the end of a paragraph as in the complaint letter to the bank. You need to weigh the style benefits of these words against the benefit of keeping your letter tight and allowing ideas to flow from one paragraph to the next. Transition words and repetition are most useful when linking paragraphs. Here is an example from the complaint letter to the bank of how to link two paragraphs using a transition phrase.

> Although I paid the amount in full, the payment was late, and as a result you gave me an *adverse credit rating*.

> I cannot begin to tell you the trouble the *adverse credit rating* has caused. Even now, despite my changed circumstances, I am unable for example to obtain a credit card.

You will notice that each sentence in these two paragraphs follows on from the previous material and points to what is ahead. Linking sentences and paragraphs in this way allows your letter to flow smoothly. Even where you do not repeat the same words and phrases, you can use particular expressions to keep the narrative flowing and link paragraphs. For example, the sentence 'Already much has happened at your instigation' invites the reader to move forward and discover what in fact has happened. At other times you will simply want to add some vital information even though you cannot link it directly to the main point you are making in your letter.

In the letter to the bank boss, I wanted to toss in the information about the working-class origins of the Commonwealth Bank because it was relevant in a general way to my complaints about the bank ignoring the needs of ordinary people. But the reality of paragraph six is that it appears from left field with no obvious links to the paragraphs before and after. In fact, you could say that nothing in this paragraph is connected with the rest of the letter. Does that mean, however, that the paragraph is out of place and obstructs the flow of the letter? Probably not. It is sufficient that a piece of vital information is linked generally with the theme and tone of your letter—adding interest and variety to your communication—but with one word of warning.

Each paragraph in your letter can probably only bear the weight of one idea. You must assume the person you are writing to is easily distracted and needs to be led by the hand through each of your ideas. Given the capacity of the human brain to take in new information, you are unlikely to lose the attention of your correspondent because of an overload of material. But how you present the material is critical to the reader remaining focused and giving your letter the attention it deserves. If you look once again at the letter to the bank boss, hopefully you will find only one idea in each paragraph. Apparently we read in paragraphs and mixing two or more ideas in one paragraph scrambles our thought processes.

Closing

The different threads in your correspondence (including any scrambled thoughts) will need to be drawn together in one or two paragraphs at the end of your letter. In the complaint letter to the bank, three points persisted to the end: the child's bank account, the bank's advertising at the cricket and the problem of the adverse credit rating. This last point was the main focus of the letter, so the last paragraph was the place to repeat and emphasise my principal complaint. But the other two points also needed to be resolved and I did this by bringing them together in the second last paragraph and using the key word 'respectable' as a link. Cricket is a respectable game, I suggested, and if the bank wishes to share in the reflected glory of cricket it must modify the harsh impact of its fees on people who cannot afford to pay.

Ending on a personal note

Most letters end on a complimentary personal note. The first letter in this book to the premier ends with the sentence 'Please give this matter your urgent and personal attention'. Of course, if you do not know the person you are writing to, and you do not want the person to do anything, a personal ending may be inappropriate. In fact, it may be counter-productive to end on a personal note, as such an ending often bears all the sincerity of the expression 'Have a nice day'. In the bank complaint letter, nothing is intended to be personal about the last paragraph, and no use is made of the personal pronoun 'you' or 'your'. Still, this is the exception to the rule, and here are a number of personal closing statements that may be helpful.

- Please give this matter your urgent and personal attention.
- Thank you once again for the good news.
- I look forward to hearing from you.
- May good fortune continue to favour your endeavours.
- Thank you for taking the time to read this letter.
- It was good to catch up with you.
- Please respond to this letter as soon as possible.
- I will be pleased to attend for an interview whenever it is convenient to you.
- I would like to thank you for the kind service and attention you have provided.
- Again, I apologise for the incorrect information for which I am entirely responsible.
- I hope you enjoyed the occasion as much as I did.
- I trust this unfortunate circumstance will not damage our friendship.
- Thank you again for your encouragement and support.
- I am returning your invoice, and when it has been amended, I will be pleased to forward my cheque.
- Please send additional information for my consideration.
- I hope my quotation will prove acceptable to the board.
- Please be assured you will be hearing from me again on this matter.
- In the circumstances I am reluctant to provide further assistance.

- My lawyer will be in touch with you about this matter.
- I trust you will excuse me for not attending.
- Please confirm our arrangements as soon as possible.
- I will be happy to call and discuss the situation if you think that will help.
- Please give my love to Clare and Megan.
- If you require further information, please let me know.
- I sincerely regret any inconvenience my late decision may have caused.

Some people enjoy writing a complimentary personal sentence at the end of a letter and running it into the complimentary close. This is a legitimate way to conclude a letter and was once quite fashionable. For example, 'This letter is written with all the love and affection of, your sincere friend'. Or, 'With my pleasant recollections and kindest regards, I remain, your sincere friend'. Apart from the flowery language, shorthand endings of this kind are actually back in vogue with the advent of email. It is now quite common to read email messages that join together a complimentary personal sentence and a complimentary close, such as 'Talk to you later, good luck' or 'Get back to me as soon as you can, all the best'.

Action statement

From the beginning to the end of the letter to the bank boss, I was hoping some action statement would present itself as a fitting conclusion to the letter. However, I was hardly in a position to ask for a credit card application as the first question on the form is: 'Do you have a good credit rating?' In the end, I could only question the bank's credit rating policy. I thought of concluding with a statement about bank closures—more than 1500 bank branches have closed in Australia in the past five years. You can get away with one extraneous paragraph in a letter, but a closing that introduces new material is out of the question, and so I decided against ending on the subject of bank closures.

Generally, you will end on an action statement—something you want your correspondent to do. If you are simply providing information, or complaining about a particular policy, you can take the opportunity to reinforce your main point by repeating it in the final paragraph.

The bank was kind enough to respond to my letter in time for the present edition of *The Book of Letters*. A nice man in customer relations named Charlie Trkulja put pen to paper, getting the dateline and salutation wrong. In the first draft of my reply— my brainstorming session—I carried on about the author's name being difficult to pronounce, and nothing personal, but running three consonants together is always a problem with the English language. Of course, this is not true—many words in English include three consonants together. It is also bad form to complain about a person's name in a multicultural society. After Israel, Australia is the most culturally diverse country in the world, and we will always be confronting names that are difficult to pronounce. To take a stand against a person's name is about as useful as railing against God so I left this out of my final version. Letter 3.2 was my reply and you will notice I finally managed to get an action statement in the last paragraph in the form of a question about the bank boss reading my letter.

3.2 Reply letter to bank

Mr Charlie Trkulja
Head of Customer Relations
Commonwealth Bank
GPO Box 2719
Sydney NSW 1155

Dear Mr. Trkulja,

You wrote to me on 17 January 2001, and I am extremely grateful for your letter. You put the date in the wrong place and the correct salutation is 'Dear Mr Breen', but overall you scored well on my letters rating scale.

If you wish to fix the salutation problem, I suggest you speak to the data entry person at the bank and instruct them to replace the complimentary title 'The Hon.' with 'Mr' or 'Ms' as the case may be. As to the date, it goes above the inside address, not below.

Six weeks have passed since I received your letter and I wonder how the investigation is going? More to the point, I wonder what you are actually investigating? The Commonwealth Bank was established in 1911, I was late paying the $1900, you reported me as a bad credit risk, you hit the child's bank account for six with bank charges and you muscled in on the cricket. Nothing controversial here, Mr Trkulja.

One matter you might investigate is whether the general manager of the bank actually got to read my letter. I would like to know for the benefit of readers of *The Book of Letters* who I am encouraging to go to the top with their complaints. You will do my cause a great service if you are able to confirm that Mr Murray did in fact read my letter and personally instructed you to write to me.

I look forward to hearing from you.

Yours sincerely,

Peter Breen

Less than a month after I wrote this letter I received a further letter from the bank, this time from the boss of Group Corporate Relations. I was told the newspaper report of the bank charging $3.40 bank fees to the child's bank account was completely inaccurate. Apparently the child's father looked at the wrong statement. The newspaper had published a retraction. As to the cricket, that was equally embarrassing. I discovered that the Commonwealth Bank Cricket Academy has produced more than sixteen graduates who represented Australia in test matches and one day internationals. The bank is also the principal sponsor of Australian Women's Cricket. In addition, the bank forgoes over $40 million in revenue each year by not applying fees to various accounts, including non-profit community group accounts and—wait for it—children's accounts. And the bad news? According to the bank's records I still owed the $1900. Correspondence is continuing.

Some hints about language

Like speaking, writing is a skill you learn, and the way to improve your skill is to practise. If you wrote several thousand letters each year your skill would improve dramatically. Good writing has the feel of a real person talking. Reading your work aloud is a good way to develop rhythm and force in your sentences. Using a conversational tone is certainly a good way to write your letters, but first you may need to eliminate some bad writing habits.

Eliminate 'which' and 'that'

The Commonwealth Bank nailed its black and yellow colours to the mast by adopting the phrase 'Which Bank?' in its marketing program. But another question, equally important, is why not 'That Bank'? The two words 'which' and 'that' are interchanged so frequently it may be impossible in many cases to work out which one is correct. Where you are deciding between different alternatives, such as 'which one' or 'which bank', then 'which' is correct. In the following two sentences, however, the differences between the two words may not be so clear cut.

The house that Jack built is that one on the corner.
The house, which Jack built, is that one on the corner.

Both sentences are correct, and any book on grammar will tell you 'that' is used to begin phrases that are essential to the meaning of a sentence, while 'which' is used to begin non-essential phrases—that is to say, phrases that simply provide additional information. If all that is a bit confusing, the good news is I only raised the 'which' and 'that' conundrum to tell you one of the best kept secrets of letter writing. Good letter writers go through their draft letters with a red pen and strike out 'that' and 'which' wherever the word can be eliminated. So our sentence becomes:

> The house Jack built is the one on the corner.

You will notice the word 'that' gives force to some sentences and should not be deleted. The trick is you only delete 'that' and 'which' when the words appear before a person's name or personal pronouns such as 'I', 'we', 'you', 'your', 'he', 'her', 'their', etc. For example, 'I told you *that* I would be late' is painful compared with 'I told you I would be late'.

Choose active verbs

Use the red pen to strike out passive verbs, particularly 'being' words like 'is' and 'are', as they can kill your writing instead of breathing life into it. Similar words to look out for include 'was', 'were', 'be', 'being' and 'been'. Phrases in the same undesirable company include 'there is', 'there are', 'there were', 'there will be', 'it is', 'it was' and 'it has been'. Read any difficult letter and count the number of times these words and phrases appear. I have reworked each of the following sentences in the active voice.

> Passive: The red pen should be used to strike out passive verbs.
> Active: Use the red pen to strike out passive verbs.

Passive: So many choices were confusing.
Active: So many choices confused me.

Active verbs give your writing energy and make it forceful. In other words, active verbs make your writing direct and immediate while passive verbs make it remote and roundabout. Sometimes a 'being' verb will give your letter immediacy, particularly if you use it at the beginning of a sentence. Personally, I quite like 'It is' and 'I am' and 'We are' at the beginning of a sentence when I am writing a rocket letter. These phrases have a certain authority—provided you are not looking for a reply. Often you will find these phrases at the beginning of a series of insults such as:

- *It is* a great pity you continue to make a fool of yourself.
- *I am* appalled that the solution to the problem remains a mystery to you.
- *We are* astounded you ignore our attempts to inform you of the situation.

Avoid 'it' and 'the'

Two words, quite harmless in themselves, have put more letters in the waste paper basket than any other single cause. I have no statistics for this grand statement, of course, and I can speak only from my own experience, but I refer to the tendency of the human brain to appear comatose following a series of sentences each beginning with the article 'The' or, worse, the article 'it'. It is enough to send the most dedicated reader on a walk in the park. 'It' is a particular problem because it refers to something said earlier that may not be immediately obvious to the reader.

After a pleasant walk in the park, our intrepid reader returned to her book, ready for the next chapter. It was something she had to do.

To avoid putting your correspondent through the guessing game, always place 'it' immediately after the word or phrase it refers to.

> After a pleasant walk in the park—she had to do it—our intrepid reader returned to her book, ready for the next chapter.

'The' is no less pervasive if you use it to begin successive sentences. Two in a row is the absolute limit, in my opinion, although technical writers will sometimes string together several sentences beginning with 'the' to describe some complex piece of equipment or esoteric theory about the meaning of life. You get the feeling 'the' is seen as a way to keep things simple, but in reality the article 'the' at the beginning of successive sentences makes reading quite difficult. The Statement of Ethics for New South Wales lawyers published by the Law Society is a case in point.

> The law should protect the rights and freedoms of members of the community. The administration of the law should be just. The lawyer practises law as an officer of the Court. The lawyer's role is both to uphold the rule of law and serve the community in the administration of justice.

Of course, nothing is simple about this statement as no link exists between each of the sentences. Without transition words and phrases, the ideas in each sentence must be considered in isolation. Somehow the Statement of Ethics needs reworking so that the central idea flows through each sentence. By limiting the use of 'the' at the beginning of successive sentences the statement becomes much more readable.

> As an officer of the Court a lawyer has two roles, one to serve the community in the administration of justice, and the other to protect the rights and freedoms of clients. The lawyer will fulfill these dual

roles by balancing the interests of clients with the need to uphold the rule of law.

Post, fax or email?

Old habits die hard with letter writing as in other aspects of life. A letter on good quality stationery, perhaps with embossed letterhead, once enjoyed special attention in the snowstorm of papers that frequently passed across my desk. These days, the only fancy stationery I see arrives from government ministers who ought to be more frugal with taxpayers' money.

Another reason for consigning pretty letters to the dustbin of history is to be found in the benefits of the information revolution. Now you can attach just about anything to an email message except good quality stationery. For critics of the Internet, the lowest common denominator in modern forms of written communication is plain white paper. Looking on the bright side, however, plain white paper is the currency of the written word throughout the world, and if you happen to own a scanner, you can reproduce photographs, paintings and illustrations to look almost, or exactly, the same as the originals. In my own experience the humble scanner opened up more of the benefits of digital information technology than any other piece of electronic equipment.

The fax machine too has changed forever the way we communicate in writing. It was originally developed by a Scottish inventor, Alexander Bain, in 1843. Apparently fax machine technology is not particularly earth shattering and Bain's invention lay dormant in a commercial sense for 130 years. By 1970 just 50 000 fax machines existed in the entire United States. The market potential for sending written messages over the telephone was realised very quickly, however, and by 1980 almost every office had a fax machine.

Some people still have trouble coming to terms with the idea you can send something in writing over the telephone, and so they send you the original letter by post after sending you a faxed copy. As well as doubling their own workload, these people hope to do the same for everybody else. Fortunately, they alert you to their sinister plan by stamping the original letter to the effect that a copy has been faxed. My advice is to consign such letters to the same dustbin described earlier.

In fact, the fax machine itself is likely to end up in the dustbin of history sooner than you might think. Emails are faster and cheaper than faxes. Once you become a regular email junkie, you will find the fax machine just clutters your office and ties up a telephone line. In the meantime you can purchase a computer program that allows you to send and receive fax messages through your computer using the same telephone line as your email.

The advantages of email are vast. You can send and receive messages almost instantly. More importantly, you can easily send a message to more than one person at a time, or you can forward on a received message to other people you want to keep in the loop. There are disadvantages however. Because of email's speed, your writing style can quickly deteriorate. Sometimes you will hit the 'Send' button before proofreading, or before considering the implications of your email. You also need to be careful about filing emails since they carry the same weight in law as mailed letters.

Recently I became involved in a dispute between two members of parliament over an alleged defamatory email sent to several journalists. Amongst other things, I said it was a pity the email had been sent. Much to my surprise, the sender informed me he could cancel those emails that had not been opened by the journalists. It turned out only two or three had been opened and the rest were somehow cancelled. I confess to not knowing myself how this is done, but I am reliably informed it is neither difficult nor uncommon to cancel an unopened email.

Personally I prefer the security of the post for confidential communications and other written material that may raise questions of defamation. Email is not a particularly secure medium and, as I said earlier, you can easily find yourself in trouble if the wrong person opens your email, or if the person you sent it to sends it on to somebody else without your permission. Another problem with email is it looks bland and sometimes the recipient will not treat your communication as seriously as a flash letter on official letterhead. The best way to deal with this problem is to use carefully chosen language instead of email shorthand.

Mind you, the tricks and shortcuts of email are not without their appeal. I have seen the idiosyncratic rules for writing emails described as 'netiquette' and some are worth mentioning. Avoid writing an email message using all capital letters as this is apparently bad form. Do not send jokes or garbage attachments to your friends, particularly at their business email address, as you could cost them their job. Do not use 'emoticons' (short for emotional icons) in business correspondence although they are fine for personal messages. Emoticons look like facial expressions if you tilt your head to the left and they include:

:-)	Smiley	:-p	Tongue-in-cheek
:-))	Very Smiley	:-*	Kissing
;-)	Winking	:-v	Shouting
:-(	Sad	:-o	Shocked
:-((	Very Sad	:-t	Angry
:-/	Undecided	:-{	Disapproving

An email does not look like an ordinary letter. The rules about the salutation and complimentary close are the same as traditional correspondence, but instead of letterhead and an inside address, an email message is preceded by a header, which contains the sender's name, recipient's name and subject matter. And your sign-off at the bottom of the message will be different, as generally you cannot handwrite your signature into an email. Instead, many people use the automatic 'signature' function included in most email programs. You can create a signature file consisting of your name, company details and other contact information.

Sending unsolicited and indiscriminate emails to people who do not know you is called 'spamming' and it is the Internet equivalent of a streaker at the cricket. Apart from making a fool of yourself, you can easily land in more trouble than you bargained for, and you are liable to be sued. Many Internet service providers have declared war on spamming and they are quite capable of ruining your business reputation overnight. Spamming is not the same as marketing to targeted email lists, however, and if you purchase a mailing list from a reputable source with the appropriate assurances about privacy laws, you may successfully expand your customer base. Marketing to legitimate email lists can be profitable and rewarding while spamming is always a disaster.

One word of warning about email. More than five million emails are sent each day in Australia, many without the permission of their authors. If you receive an email, do not forward it on to somebody else without the author's permission, otherwise you are in breach of the copyright laws. In the same vein, if you put written material on your website without the permission of the author, again you have a problem with copyright. Laws protecting an author's moral rights, as well as laws intended to prevent the spread of computer viruses, are now in force throughout Australia. If you think this is a trifling matter, maximum penalties of five years in gaol or fines of up to $60 000 apply for serious breaches of these laws.

This concludes Part One of the book. I trust you will practise your letter writing skills until a couple of thousand letters each year is a breeze. Part Two of the book is intended to give you new ideas about what to say in your letters. 'Letters for every occasion' may seem like a bold claim, but I am confident you

will find a precedent for just about any situation you are likely to encounter in your letter writing. If you do strike an unusual situation and none of the precedent letters in Part Two appear suitable, write to me at the postal address shown at the back of the book and I may be able to send you a sample letter from the WriteQuick program.

Part Two

LETTERS FOR EVERY OCCASION

Chapter Four

Defamation

Protecting reputations

If I were in charge of protecting reputations I would put a new broom through our defamation laws. I see no reason why the justice system should support titanic struggles about ego and money. The role of the court should be limited to deciding whether a person has been defamed. It would then be a relatively simple matter for a damages assessment panel to work out the level of monetary compensation against certain clearly defined benchmarks. In New South Wales we are already going down the defamation law reform track thanks to the efforts of former Independent Member for the South Coast, John Hatton, who successfully lobbied for civil juries to be taken off defamation cases once they decide the question whether certain imputations are defamatory. The next step is to set up a damages assessment panel.

Many people I know are cynical about defamation laws, regarding them as just another way for the rich and powerful to abuse the justice system. Over the years stories have emerged about politicians and people in business doing deals which are settled in the defamation courts on terms not to be disclosed.

Abuses of this kind are impossible to police and bring discredit on the courts. Even in cases where people have legitimate grievances, often the damage done to their reputations bears no relationship to the truckload of money they receive as compensation.

Some politicians are quite shameless about boosting their private incomes through the defamation courts. Former Prime Minister Bob Hawke was known to brag on national television about the material benefits the proceeds of defamation had brought him. In the comically named case of *Abbott & Costello v Random House Publishers*, two federal politicians relied on university scuttlebutt about one of their wives to get money from a publisher. Author Bob Ellis won this case so far as I am concerned with the memorable line, 'I would not do this to my wife even for a million dollars.'

Apart from politicians, defamation laws are also popular with lawyers. The largest award for damages was made to an American lawyer, Vic Feazell, who received US$58 million from a Texas television station for the imputation that he was a liar and a cheat. An Australian lawyer, John Marsden, holds the record for the longest and most expensive defamation case in history. Proceedings ended in 2001 after five years in the defamation courts and $12 million in legal fees. The case involved allegations of underage gay sex broadcast on the Channel Seven television network in Sydney. Although the plaintiff won the case, publicity about his promiscuous sex life and false allegations that he was a paedophile, caused extraordinary damage to his reputation. He received a damages award of $525 000, including aggravated damages since the defence was unable to prove justification— that the defamation was substantially true.

In other words, if you argue that what you have said is true, and your argument fails, you have, in effect, repeated your defamatory statements, severely aggravating the damage done to the plaintiff. As happened in the Marsden case, newspaper and

IT'S THE TRUTH I FIND MOST HURTFUL!

television reports about the trial caused far greater injury to the plaintiff than the original defamatory remarks on television. During the trial he was spat on and verbally abused in public, his property was damaged, he received threats, suffered psychological injury and his business dropped by one-third. At the time of writing Channel Seven has appealed the decision and obtained a stay order to the effect that it may withhold payment of the plaintiff's costs until the appeal is heard. The damages award has been paid.

Sometimes, defamatory remarks about people with marginal reputations are more harmful than similar comments concerning someone we know is pure and chaste. Not so long ago, a suburban newspaper published an article about pollution problems caused by manufacturing industries discharging effluent into a river. The newspaper described an industrialist who operated along the river as having been charged and heavily fined by the Pollution Control Authority, when in fact the person had been acquitted of the charge of polluting the river. A third party reading about the hapless industrialist would presume that he is at least partly responsible for the pollution problem, and the erroneous article in the newspaper is all the 'proof' the third party needs. Damage is therefore greater because you are entitled to protect even a marginal reputation. In the case referred to, Letter 4.1 was forwarded to the publishers of the defamatory material.

When the editorial manager of the newspaper receives Letter 4.1, she must choose either to ignore the letter or publish a retraction, correction or apology. If the newspaper ignores the letter and subsequently the author can prove the defamation, then failure to respond to the letter may be an aggravation of damages. If, on the other hand, the newspaper writes a retraction, correction or apology, this may be an admission of liability. Either way the newspaper loses. You are entitled to institute proceedings for damages to your reputation whether or not a reply is received to your complaint letter.

For the person defamed, perhaps the most important question to consider in deciding whether or not to commence proceedings is the question of cost. The cost of bringing a defamation case is outrageously high, mainly because of the complexity of defamation laws. You should consider carefully the extent of the damages you have suffered before commencing proceedings. Unless the damages are substantial and the defamation unquestionable, a wise man or woman will be satisfied with an apology.

If you are on the receiving end of a letter alleging defamation, you are faced with the difficult choice of ignoring the letter and possibly aggravating damages, or writing a response and admitting liability. If what you have said is clearly defamatory, but not much damage has been done, it is probably best to apologise in general terms. Although you may be admitting liability, your letter has the effect of reducing damages should the person defamed commence proceedings. Another factor in deciding whether to apologise is the effect of your apology on the person

4.1 Letter alleging defamation

Ms A. Libel
Editorial Manager
Badpress Publications
93 Press Parade
BROADSHEET HILL STA 29333

Dear Ms Libel,

I refer to an article appearing in the December issue of the *Monthly Blurb* under the heading 'Manufacturing Industries Pollute River'. In that article it is stated that I was charged and fined by the Pollution Control Authority in respect of an offence relating to the discharge of effluent into the local river. That statement is not correct, and you must be aware that I was acquitted of the charge brought by the Authority.

My reputation has been greatly damaged by the incorrect statement in your publication, and I wonder whether you can offer some explanation for your conduct. Although it is doubtful how far a retraction, correction or apology can go to remedy the matter, I request that the appropriate action be taken.

I look forward to your reply.

Yours faithfully,
Riverbank Manufacturing Company

John Smith
Managing Director

hurt by your defamatory remarks. A reasonable person will generally accept the apology and move on, even though some basis for a legal action may exist. Assuming you are dealing with a reasonable person and you wish to avoid paying for a lawyer, Letter 4.2 may be helpful.

4.2   Letter of apology

Mr John Smith
Managing Director
Riverbank Manufacturing Company
27 Reputation Parade
RIVERBANK STA 24331

Dear Mr Smith,

I refer to your letter regarding an article appearing in the December issue of the *Monthly Blurb* under the heading 'Manufacturing Industries Pollute River'.

On receipt of your letter I immediately checked the matter and found that your observation is correct. The article incorrectly described you as having been charged and fined by the Pollution Control Authority in respect of an offence relating to the discharge of effluent into the local river.

I unreservedly apologise for any damage that may have been done as a result of the error in the article. I also undertake to publish an apology in the next issue of the *Monthly Blurb* and to take any further action you may reasonably require to remedy the error. You should indicate your requirements, if any, by return post.

Yours sincerely,
Badpress Publications

A. Libel

A. Libel (Ms)
Editorial Manager

If you are in any doubt as to the extent of the damage done by your defamatory publication, you should seek advice before replying to any letter from the person defamed or their representative. A decision either to admit liability and reduce the damages, or to ignore the letter and risk aggravating the situation, is one for a suitably qualified lawyer if the damages may be substantial.

A question of slander

To defame someone in a permanent form such as a letter is libel
while defamatory speech is slander. So the statements that John
Smith is said to be 'good, but very slow' or 'thorough, but very
expensive' or 'smart, but can't run a business' or even 'bloody
hopeless' are all slanderous even though they may be true, and
you may want to use Letter 4.3 to put the record straight to the
person responsible.

4.3   Letter alleging slander

Ms Ava Bittosay
26 Imputation Drive
STOREYVILLE STA 23908

Dear Ms Bittosay,

Last Friday, it was reported to me that you described me to Bill
Brown as 'good, but very slow', a statement that imputes to me a
dilatory attitude to my work and disregard for normal business
efficiency. My reputation has been damaged as a result of this
slanderous statement, and Bill Brown has cause to question the way
in which I have attended to his work. I am now obliged to demonstrate
to him that I have acted efficiently and properly. This has put me
to considerable expense and embarrassment.

Although it is doubtful how far a correction, retraction or apology
can go to remedy the unquestionable damage to my reputation, I
request that the appropriate action be taken as quickly as possible
to mitigate the damage.

Yours faithfully,

O. Fended

O. Fended (Mr)

If you are in Ms Bittosay's position, again you need to be
careful about your response to this letter. Ignoring the letter could

amount to an aggravation of damages while the most suppliant reply may be an admission of liability. As to the monetary compensation to which you may be entitled for defamatory statements, I know an engineer who was awarded $15 000 damages in a defamation case when a former customer told several of the engineer's other customers he was a hopeless engineer and they should do business elsewhere. Many of us are guilty of these slanderous remarks from time to time, and if you get caught with your foot in your mouth, I would recommend Letter 4.4 if you wish to make an unqualified apology.

4.4 Letter of apology for slander

Mr O. Fended
13 Inference Avenue
ACTIONTOWN STA 25111

Dear Mr Fended,

You have complained that certain remarks I made damaged your reputation. I confess that I made the remarks under an entire misapprehension as to the facts. I hereby unreservedly withdraw every statement made by me which may in any way be said to reflect on your character and the quality of your work.

I admit that the remarks had no basis in fact and I deeply regret making them. I hereby tender my sincere apology and I trust you will accept this apology in the spirit in which it is offered. Please be assured I will not make similar remarks again.

Yours faithfully,

A. Bittosay

Ava Bittosay

You will notice this letter stops short of admitting liability for damages, even though it is a generous apology. An admission of liability might be the addition of the words 'and I hope you will accept this apology as the best amends I can make for the injury and annoyance I have caused'. These words would preclude you from arguing subsequently that your defamatory remarks did not cause any damage. At the risk of repeating myself, if you have any doubts about the likely consequences of your slanderous remarks, make sure you get advice before responding to a complaint. If your response is the only evidence of liability, it may be an expensive letter, and the lawyer's fees will be cheap by comparison.

Nothing much turns on the difference between libel and slander. Both are defamatory and entitle an aggrieved person to take action for damages to their reputation. Statements made on radio or television are regarded as libel because they are recorded in permanent form. A defamatory statement made over the telephone would normally be slander unless the conversation were recorded. Slander is more difficult to prove than libel as the nuances in the spoken word are lost once the defamatory material is committed to writing. For this reason you might want to think twice about repeating your seemingly innocuous verbal remarks in a letter, even a letter of apology.

Parts of a defamation

The first part of a defamation is the publication of your words to a person other than the person defamed. If a defamatory letter to the manager of a company is opened by a secretary or clerk in the ordinary course of their job, the reading of that letter constitutes its publication. This is so even if you did not know that the letter would be opened by a person other than the addressee. Therefore, address your letter to your victim by name and mark the letter and envelope 'Private', 'Confidential' or 'Personal'. If it is then opened by somebody else, you are not responsible. When you send a defamatory email, make sure it can be accessed only by the person you are writing to.

The second part of a defamation is that the actual defamation is not the words you choose, but the meanings or imputations they convey. It seems that just about every word in the English language has a number of meanings, and so you must be precise. Choose your words so you will convey only the meaning you are prepared to justify. An exaggerated example, but one that will give you my general drift, is that it would be wiser to write that a car salesman sold you a defective vehicle than to say he sold you a 'bomb'. Or, do not say he is 'bad' when you really mean he was rude to you. If you wish to say that Mrs Murphy's biscuits taste awful, say so. Do not say they are 'poisonous'. The possible examples are endless and have provided entertainment for the courts and easy money for lawyers for centuries.

Having just advised you to be precise, I must immediately contradict myself and say you must also know when to be vague. For a person to be defamed they must be identified as the target of your correspondence. However, simply not naming somebody will not help you if you have included sufficient details in your letter for any reasonable reader, having some knowledge of the person, to readily identify them. It is, however, not possible to defame a group unless the group is sufficiently small that your slighting reference to it could be taken as referring to each individual member. Shakespeare was quite safe when he wrote 'the first thing we'll do is kill all the lawyers', whereas the journalist who wrote how 'lawyer X mistreated her clients' suffered severely. To take another example, if you were to write of a named company that it was run by a bunch of idiots, you may well be defaming the individual members of the board.

Who can be defamed?

Defamation is normally a personal action, but any body or association that is capable at law of commencing any proceedings may be defamed. Companies regularly sue, and even trade unions have been held to be capable of suing. For example, you might say that thousands of dollars of the funds of a certain named trade union are wagered every Saturday at the races. Not only would you be likely to defame the union's treasurer and perhaps other union officials personally, but there is a likelihood that the union itself would be entitled to sue because the statement is of a nature that would be likely to damage the union's effectiveness as a union.

Despite views to the contrary, you are entitled to speak ill of the dead anywhere in Australia. In doing so, you must be careful to avoid sideswiping a living person in the process. For example, to say of a dead person 'he was such a philanderer he never found time for his wife' could impute illegitimacy to his living children and adultery to his living wife. Another way in which it is possible to unintentionally sideswipe another on your way to your true target is by being too general in your identification of the person you are writing about. This is the reverse of what I have said above on the subject of knowing when to be vague.

One of the largest awards of damages in the history of Australian defamation went to an architect and his company for a cartoon depicting a building designed by the plaintiffs and suggesting they were inhuman and anti-social. At the trial the newspaper disavowed its intention of injuring either the designer of the building or his company. All this was to no avail. The newspaper should have been more precise in identifying the object of its humour. The moral here for letter writers is that if you are writing to complain about somebody, identify the person by name, otherwise your unkind remarks could apply to a third party without you realising the person might be offended.

Available defences

If you think that this brief outline of the law relating to defamation is complicated, I should tell you that the defences available are even more convoluted, and they vary from State to State to Territory. The most common is the defence of truth, the refuge of all ardent letter writers. What must be proved to be true is the meanings your letter conveys. Also, truth alone is not always a defence. In some States and Territories you must also prove whether the letter related to a matter of public interest, or was written on a privileged occasion, or that it was sent for the public benefit. Obviously there is no public benefit in telling your next door neighbour that the lady across the street has formed a liaison with the milkman, not even if the affair is playing havoc with your milk deliveries. The information must be a matter of sufficient importance to warrant the resulting damage to a person's reputation. It would probably be to the public benefit to notify the manager of a business that one of their employees had tried to sell you information confidential to the business.

The other major defence to a defamation action is your right to an opinion or comment. What distinguishes a statement of fact from an expression of opinion or a comment can be a very difficult matter. Frequently it is a fine line, but a comment is an expression of a person's view or opinion based on statements of fact, either contained in the letter or which are notorious. For example, to say 'X is a thief' cannot be other than a statement of fact. But, to say 'I've seen X in the supermarket twice now taking items off the shelf and placing them down his shirt front and walking out with them and, in my opinion, he is a thief' is an entirely different matter. I can hear you muttering already that all cases are not so clear cut, and that is just the point—in your letters they must be.

Limitations exist on comment. The subject matter must be one of public interest, and the view expressed must be an opinion honestly held by the person expressing it. If, therefore, you wish to write of a person that he or she is a rogue, an impostor or a quack and that represents your honest opinion, then spell out the facts and make sure you have them correct. It should be clear from your letter that your expression of opinion is based on those facts and that it is an expression of opinion. You might follow the statements of fact with words such as 'Having weighed all the facts set out above, I have formed the opinion that X is a thief, but you of course will draw your own conclusion'.

Chapter Five

Overcharging

Professional services

It costs more these days to have your washing machine repaired at home than it does to have a lawyer prepare your will or a doctor save your life. You may have a point of view about the injustice or otherwise of this situation, no doubt depending on your own employment. My feeling is we live in a consumer-based society and therefore we must pay the cost of maintaining consumer goods. In addition, my knowledge of mechanical matters is so thin I have no choice—when the washing machine breaks down, either I call a washing machine repairer or I take my clothes to the laundromat.

As for doctors and lawyers and other professionals such as surveyors and dentists, technological developments in the past twenty years have brought the incomes of many of these people back to the rest of the field. Today we find less demand for medical services because we are healthier, less demand for accountants (prior to the GST at any rate) because of computers, less demand for surveyors because of simplified title to land, less demand for dentists because of fluoride in our water systems, and the list goes on. Most professionals recognise that we live in a changing world and they are fairly philosophical about the fall in demand for their services. A few unscrupulous types are about, however, who intentionally overcharge you in an attempt to restore lost incomes, and others who overcharge you without realising it.

All professionals are bound by scales of charges and they cannot charge you above the scales without first obtaining your consent. In other words, if you consult professional people and their accounts exceed the scale of charges provided by their governing bodies, they are in breach of the rules and may be guilty of professional misconduct. That having been said, there are some circumstances in which a professional person can charge above the scale of charges, so you should make some discreet enquiries before assuming you have been robbed. An agreement may exist entitling the person to charge above scale. Check with the governing body of the professional concerned to find out what you should pay. Medical specialists, for example, charge different fees depending upon whether they work in public or private hospitals.

When you receive a bill and you feel that the bill is excessive, the first thing to do is approach the person who sent it to find out how the account has been calculated. Most professionals charge less, in fact, than they might be entitled to, and will happily give you an explanation of their account. Try to avoid upsetting the person, as you could get a new bill for more than the previous bill. If you do not know the person very well, or you are reluctant to speak about the account, you can write a nice letter in the form of Letter 5.1 which simply asks a question of the person who provided the services.

5.1   Fee inquiry letter

Ms Penny Nice
General Manager
Nice Professional Services
27 Ethical Drive
INTEGRITY HILL STA 21044

Dear Ms Nice,

I refer to your recent attendances during my illness/divorce/fight with the Taxation Department. May I take this opportunity to thank you for your prompt and courteous attention to my problem, and to assure you that I will be pleased to consult you or recommend you in the future should the need arise.

One small matter I would like to clarify concerns a commercial and not a personal matter. I would be obliged if you could inform me of the basis on which you have rendered your account, particularly having regard to the recommended fee for similar services provided by the governing body of your profession.

I look forward to your reply.

Yours sincerely,

I. M. Well.

I. M. Well (Mr)

You will notice that the phrase 'particularly having regard to the recommended fee for similar services provided by the governing body of your profession' is delightfully vague, but it does place an obligation on the professional person to explain the fees. Most professionals will reply to your letter with a statement of the recommended fee, and you will be invited to compare that fee with the fee you have been charged. Hopefully, both figures will be the same. If you have been charged above the recommended fee, there may be some reasonable explanation. The job may have involved an unusual amount of skill, extra time may have been spent on the job, or it may have required some urgent priority. Also, many professionals are in the privileged position that the market recognises their expertise, and they charge accordingly. You may not agree with this practice, but it is a fact of life in a free market, and you need to enter fee arrangements with your eyes wide open.

When you have been charged above a recommended fee by a professional your only redress may be that the professional should have told you the amount of their fee before providing the service. In such a case it would be reasonable to pay only the recommended fee. The governing bodies of some professions set prescribed fees (as distinct from recommended fees) for many items of work. Clearly, a professional is not entitled to charge in excess of a prescribed fee. If you are in any doubt about the work being undertaken by the professional, check with them or the governing body of the profession, and you will be told whether or not the work is covered by prescribed fees or recommended fees. Do this before the work is undertaken and you may save yourself a good deal of wrangling afterwards.

Professional people are more amenable to discussion about their fees before undertaking work. If it is work covered by prescribed fees, the discussion will be short and sweet. If a professional person is charging a recommended fee, try to commit them to that fee irrespective of the nature or complexity of the job. The negotiations are no different from similar negotiations with somebody about to fix your lawnmower or washing machine. Generally, professionals will not charge below recommended fees unless there is a special reason to do so, otherwise they can be accused of attracting business unfairly. When you receive a bill from a professional which you know is in excess of a prescribed fee, the person should be told and an explanation sought. Letter 5.2 may be useful.

5.2   Fee complaint letter

Mr U. R. Nasty
General Manager
Nasty Professional Services
29 Unethical Drive
INTEGRITY HILL STA 21044

Dear Mr Nasty,

I refer to your recent attendances during my illness/divorce/fight with the Taxation Department. May I take this opportunity to thank you for your prompt and courteous attention to my problem, and to assure you that I will be pleased to consult you or recommend you in the future, should the need arise.

One small matter I should like to clarify concerns a commercial and not a personal matter. I am under the impression that the governing body of your profession has set a prescribed fee for the service you have provided, but your account indicates a charge in excess of that prescribed fee. I would be obliged if you could itemise your account to enable me to give the matter further consideration.

I look forward to your reply.

Yours sincerely,

I. M. Notwell

I. M. Notwell (Mr)

The explanation you receive for the charge in excess of the prescribed fee may well be special skill, unusual complexity, extra time required, urgent priority or some such fairytale. Do not accept this explanation. 'Prescribed fee' means what it says, unless you have agreed in advance with the professional to pay something other than the prescribed fee. Make sure you closely read the terms of any written fee arrangement, and get advice if you have any doubts about the meaning of the contract. A few hundred dollars spent before you sign the contract may save you many thousands down the track.

Consumer services

Most consumer service charges are set by prevailing market conditions, and unless you know something of the market, you will have no idea whether you are being overcharged or not. The best way to find out about the market is to shop around. Telephone the services department of the manufacturer of the item you want repaired, and find out the standard or average price for fixing it. Unfortunately, most repairers will not give you a quotation without first charging you for a service call, and once they arrive with their tools, it may take just a few minutes to fix the problem. It is rarely worth your while to get a second quote, and in the end the best price and the best job are usually provided by the person most helpful on the telephone.

With larger repair jobs where the account is likely to be more than a thousand dollars, it is wise to get a written quotation before any work is undertaken. This quote will be your only protection if you get involved in a dispute as to the cost of the work or standard of workmanship. If the quote is verbal, or written and not detailed, you should write a letter to the contractor or repairer setting out the terms of your arrangement. No particular form of words is needed so long as you put the main points in writing. Letter 5.3 is a good starting point.

5.3   Letter confirming quote

Mr S. O. Cold
General Manager
Ice Cold Refrigeration Company
34 Frozen Way
CHILLY HILL STA 22440

Dear Mr Cold,

I refer to your quote for the repair of my refrigerator and note you are willing to undertake the following repairs:

- replace broken freezer tray
- repair or replace freezer door
- re-gas freezer bottles
- repair or replace thermostat
- recondition motor
- replace rubber door seals

I accept your quote of $1000 and enclose a cheque for the deposit of $100 as requested.

I note also you are willing to guarantee parts and workmanship for a period of three months from the date on which you complete the work. You expect a completion date not later than 31 January next.

Yours sincerely,

Y. Repair

Y. Repair (Ms)

A copy of this letter will be invaluable if you subsequently argue with the contractor or repairer as to what he was supposed to do, how much he was going to charge, the extent of his guarantee and when the job was to be completed. Payment of a deposit with the letter is a good idea because if the contractor has cashed the cheque then you do not need to prove that the contractor received the letter, but as an added precaution you might ask the contractor to sign and return a duplicate of the letter. The important thing is to get the terms of your arrangement into writing because without the writing you have nothing going for you when the refrigerator breaks down five minutes after the repair job is completed. You can adapt this letter to make it relevant to renovations to your house, repairs to your car, painting the office or even the installation of a new computer. One useful adaptation is Letter 5.4 to your computer company.

5.4   Further letter confirming quote

Mr H. Shot
General Manager
Hot Shot Computer Services
161 Data Drive
COMPUTER VALLEY STA 26339

Dear Mr Shot,

Re: Installation of Model 874E Computer

I refer to your quote for the installation of the above computer in my premises and note that the computer is to perform the following functions:

- Record GST and Business Activity Statement
- Create debtors' ledger
- Create creditors' ledger
- Perform budget and cash flow forecasts
- Print cheques and receipts
- Maintain cash book

I accept your quote of $2500 which will include training a member of my staff in the use of the computer.

Also, I note you are willing to guarantee all software and hardware for a period of two (2) years from the date of installation, that being a date not later than 31 May next.

Kindly acknowledge receipt of this letter by signing and returning the attached duplicate.

Yours sincerely,
Model T. Industries

E. Manual System

E. Manual System
Managing Director

In this case it would not be appropriate to send a deposit, but you have asked the computer company to sign and return a duplicate of the letter, which is normal business practice. This will preclude the company from saying in any subsequent dispute that it did not receive your letter.

I cannot emphasise strongly enough the importance of writing a letter or making some other written agreement when dealing with people who have a monopoly of information, such as the repairer or the computer company. You will find that much of the mystique attaching to consumer goods disappears when you extract the essential information you need from the people you are dealing with and then convert it to plain English in the form of a letter confirming the arrangements. You will also find that the number of arguments you have is dramatically reduced, and when something cannot be resolved, you will at least be on an equal footing in terms of your bargain instead of being disadvantaged by your lack of technical information.

Lawyers' fees

Something more needs to be said about one group of professionals whose fee arrangements defy all the rules of the natural order including both gravity and justice. Like the law itself, lawyers' fees are unnecessarily complex. Any dispute about fees is almost always resolved in favour of the lawyers when you consult the Law Society or Bar Association because the governing bodies of the legal profession are also their trade unions. If you challenge the fees in court you will be confronted by a judge who looks like a lawyer, sounds like a lawyer and understands the fee arrangements but from a lawyer's point of view. In the celebrated case of the lawyer Cedric Symonds, a single judge ruled that Mr Symonds' fees were manifestly unjust, but three judges on appeal decided that because the unjust arrangement was made in writing, the client should pay.

The client was a woman involved in a Family Court property dispute with her husband. She went to the Law Society for a reference to a solicitor with family law skills. The Law Society gave her three names, including that of Cedric Symonds, and the woman prayed for guidance as to which one she should choose. Mr Symonds received the divine nod and set about drawing up a costs agreement that included photocopying at $12 per page. At the end of the dispute, the woman was awarded property valued at $681 000. Unbelievably, her legal bill was $456 000. As Richard Ackland said in the *Sydney Morning Herald*, God works in mysterious ways.

Although lawyers are required to have costs agreements with their clients where the value of the work exceeds $750, Cedric Symonds proved that a written contract is no guarantee you will not be robbed. Make sure you get advice about the costs agreement before you sign it. In the case of legal work in the federal courts, ring the Legal Costs Advisory Committee in the Attorney-General's Department at Canberra. In the States and Territories, check with the legal ombudsman or legal services commissioner—somebody independent from the governing bodies of the legal profession. The costs agreement will almost certainly read like a manuscript from the Dead Sea Scrolls, so find out what it means. This is one area of the law where statutory measures to protect law consumers have in fact had the opposite effect, and you can almost guarantee that the costs agreement is unfairly weighted in favour of the lawyer.

The New South Wales Law Reform Commission frequently undertakes reviews of the conduct and discipline of the legal profession. One area of legal practice requiring serious review, however, is the method of costing legal services and the inequities of the standard costs agreement. At present you are charged in units of ten or fifteen minutes for particular items of work. A telephone call might take two minutes, but under the present regime, you are charged a full unit—ten or fifteen minutes, depending on the item weighting. Lawyers seek to justify this practice in many different ways such as the added time it takes to open your file and record the telephone call. In reality, there can be no justification for cheating, and lawyers are being taken out of the loop in many areas of legal practice because of their fees.

Once the costs agreement is signed you are not locked into the arrangement if you decide you do not like the colour of the lawyer's eyes or he or she seems to be robbing you blind. You can terminate the arrangement at any time and ask for a final bill. You might decide to engage a new lawyer or conduct the case yourself. The lawyer has a lien on your file until the bill is paid, but the legal ombudsman or legal services commissioner may negotiate a part payment to release the file until the fees dispute is resolved. Or the lawyer may agree to release the file if you write Letter 5.5 as soon as you receive the final bill.

5.5 Letter disputing fees

Mr S. O. Good
Managing Partner
Just & Fair Law Partnership
999 Justice Avenue
EUREKA HILL STA 27444

Dear Mr Good,

Thank you for your final account for fees indicating an amount due to you of $2500.

I dispute the amount claimed both in relation to the number and length of attendances, and also the quality of your work. You have interpreted our costs agreement in a way that was not made clear when the document was signed.

As you know, I will need my file to continue the case and in the circumstances I am prepared to pay half the amount claimed in return for the file. The balance will be paid only after independent assessment of your account and mediation.

Please indicate your response as a matter of urgency so that the case is not compromised. If I do not hear from you within seven (7) days I will consult the legal ombudsman/legal services commissioner without further notice.

Yours sincerely,

A. Justinian (Ms)

Where your final bill is $2500 or less, the legal ombudsman or legal services commissioner will mediate with the lawyer and give you an independent assessment of the bill. Most complaints about lawyers relate to their fees so you are not breaking new ground with your dispute. If the bill exceeds $2500 you are at the mercy of the Supreme Court Costs Assessment Scheme. Personally, I have never been involved in a costs dispute involving the scheme, but I believe the process denies fundamental principles of natural justice. The costs assessor is another lawyer, so you do not have the benefit of an independent forum to argue your case. Furthermore, you can only communicate with the costs assessor by post, which means you do not have the right to be heard. If the post is delayed, for example, and you fail to take issue with the costs assessment, the lawyer can sign judgment against you for the amount of the assessment without further notice.

Perhaps the most disturbing feature of the costs assessment regime is that the client never has the opportunity to question the quality of the lawyer's work. Indeed, the client may be left wondering whether the lawyer actually performed much of the work for which payment is claimed. If you file for a review of the costs assessment, the lawyer's bill goes before two other costs assessors—two more brick walls from the client's point of view. Meanwhile, you must pay the costs assessors' fees for the review. You can appeal the assessment to the Supreme Court but that will cost you another $1000. This unjust system for checking a lawyer's bill is long overdue for review. Unscrupulous lawyers inflate their bills to allow for any reductions in the costs assessment process while consumers are left wondering whether they might be better advised to undertake their own legal work.

One alternative avenue for disputing lawyers' fees pending a review of the present regime is the Fair Trading Tribunal. It was never intended for this purpose, but a standard costs agreement is so manifestly unjust that members of the tribunal are reluctant

to turn away genuine consumer claims. Provided the fees involved in the dispute with your lawyer are less than $25 000, you can bring a case in the Fair Trading Tribunal on the basis that the quality of the lawyer's work was so poor you are entitled to compensation. You will ask the tribunal to make an award for the amount of the lawyer's bill. If you are successful, the bill is covered by the amount of compensation, and one debt is cancelled by the other. A feature of the Fair Trading Tribunal for claims under $10 000 is no legal representatives are allowed so you and the lawyer appear on equal terms and get to eyeball each other. This unusual experience for the lawyer will often greatly enhance the prospects of settlement.

Chapter Six

Neighbours

Nuisance

If you need any convincing about the potential problems you might have with you neighbours, think about a simple case of rainwater flowing from your land to your neighbour's land, and your neighbour complaining that the water is carrying topsoil into her garage. In order to relieve the situation, your neighbour comes onto your land and digs a trench across your backyard to divert the water. That may sound outrageous, but I know three separate instances of it happening. Letter 6.1 is a restrained letter to the neighbour in this difficult circumstance.

6.1 Water damage letter

Ms A. Party
Residents Action Committee
Placid Apartments
84 Peaceful Place
SCENIC WATERS STA 29222

Dear Ms Party,

For the past several months a problem has arisen in that rainwater during heavy storms is apparently carrying topsoil from my land to your garage, and you are concerned as to the likely damage to your property.

While I am sympathetic to the problem and have taken steps to relieve it by planting ground-cover vegetation, there is very little more I can do, and I draw your attention to the following:

1. The capacity of your drainage would appear to be inadequate having regard to the natural topography of the land.

2. Improvements to your land including rock gardens and footpaths adversely affect the natural course of water and contribute to the problem.

3. The construction of a drainage system on my land may create certain liabilities on my part should the system fail to operate effectively.

4. You are not entitled to trespass on my land to alter the natural course of water, or for any other purpose, and I ask that you desist from such activity in the future.

I sincerely hope this letter will not cause any animosity between us as we have enjoyed congenial relations in the past.

Yours truly,

U. N. Happy (Mr)

Before assuming you bear no responsibility for the topsoil washing into your neighbour's garage, make sure you have not altered the natural watercourse on your property. If you have retaining walls, drains and buildings that divert rain and storm-water to your neighbour's land, you may be liable—the legal term is 'in nuisance'—for the resulting damage to the garage. You can also be sued for nuisance if the damage is caused by some natural occurrence on your land which you caused or did not try to prevent. Water damage caused by irrigation systems, overflowing drains and artificial watercourses are classic examples of private nuisance.

Another form of private nuisance might be an ambitious gardener who uses excessive amounts of garden manure and other composting material. The gardener will do well in the local flower show and gardening competition, but the neighbours may take an entirely different view about the smells emanating from the garden and the flies and insects it attracts. Assessing the claims of adjoining land owners in this situation is a difficult balancing act. If you wish to bring the issues to a head, Letter 6.2, in response to a demand from your local council, is certain to get a reaction.

6.2   Garden mulch letter

Mr A. N. Armanaleg
Chief Planning Officer
Grassroots Local Council
66 Southern Cross Way
GRASSROOTS VALLEY STA 27555

Dear Mr Armanaleg,

I refer to the compliance notice delivered to my husband today by your health officer regarding the use of horse manure on my property as garden mulch. According to the notice, my husband and I are in breach of Council's health regulations. I have also received a claim for damages on the basis of private nuisance.

You may not be aware that the manure is fully composted before it is applied to my garden. Any suggestion that the composted material is a health hazard is rejected. The claim that it provides a medium for flies and other insects to breed is quite wrong.

My property is located in a rural area where many farm animals live in close proximity to my garden. Manure from these animals is much more likely to be the breeding place for the insect plague you say has descended on my neighbours.

For the past month I have closely monitored the garden for any signs of breeding flies and insects. I have also obtained an independent report from a horticulturist. A copy is attached. You will see from the report that there is no problem with the garden mulch and I ask that you withdraw the compliance notice as soon as possible.

Yours faithfully,

A. Forthright

A. M. Forthright (Ms)

As a matter of interest, this letter was used as a guide by a resident on the North Coast to successfully resist the local council's request for compliance. An action by the adjoining owner against the resident for private nuisance also failed in the local court. Apart from private nuisance, you can also sue for public nuisance if you are part of a group of people suffering from unreasonable interference with your comfort and convenience.

You can sue the government for creating a public nuisance but it may be able to plead the defence of statutory authority. This defence is available where the government is carrying out public work under legislation and the nuisance is an inevitable consequence of the work. The defence of statutory authority will fail, however, where some other way of doing the work is available that does not create a public nuisance. A claim against a public authority for public nuisance is likely to be an expensive and difficult action and it should be regarded as the last card in the legal pack.

Dividing fences

One neighbourhood dispute in which a letter is not only desirable but essential concerns the resolution of conflicts about dividing fences. A dispute about your fence is one area of the law where the requirement to send a letter is not negotiable. State and Territory legislation includes standard forms or letters that must be used when you write to your neighbour. If the fence between your property and that of your neighbour is inadequate, you should write to your neighbour and send a copy of the quote for repairing or replacing the fence before undertaking any work. Use Letter 6.3 as a guide after checking that it complies with your local dividing fences legislation.

6.3   Dividing fence letter

Mr Con Genial
94 Peaceful Place
PLACID LAKE STA 22688

Dear Con,

I refer to our recent discussions and confirm the quote from Ace Fencing Contractors of $1420 to repair/replace/construct the fence between our adjoining properties. A copy of the quote is attached. The contractor suggests a timber paling fence two metres high which is consistent with other fences in the area.

If the quote is acceptable please sign and return the duplicate of this letter. I propose we bear the cost equally. Under the Dividing Fences Act you are entitled to obtain an alternative quote, although I must say I tried several other contractors who wanted more money for the job. Also, Ace seems to have a good reputation.

I am not entitled under the Dividing Fences Act to undertake the work without your approval. If you do not accept the Ace quote or fail to provide an alternative quote, I am obliged to seek an order from the Local Court for the work to be done. This may require an appearance before a magistrate.

I hope you will find the Ace quote satisfactory and I look forward to your reply.

Yours sincerely,

J Nextdoor

I. M. Nextdoor (Ms)

Each State and Territory will have different rules about proving delivery of this letter and the time allowed to your neighbour to respond. Check with the local court and ask whether the Dividing Fences Act has any prescribed forms that need to be used. Whatever you do, avoid undertaking the work without your neighbour's approval, even if you are willing to bear the cost of the fence yourself. You cannot do the work without entering on your neighbour's land, and if they do not approve of the work, you are trespassing. Think twice about trespassing as your neighbour is entitled to call the police and have you removed. You can also be sued as a trespasser for any damage you cause to your neighbour's property.

Disputes frequently occur about the design of a dividing fence. Any unusual design will need to be approved by the local council and this process provides an opportunity to object to the design. Council will consider the design, standard of construction, height and material used for similar fences in the area before approving the work. If council approves an unusual design the person aggrieved can ask the neighbour who wants a fancy fence to bear the additional cost of construction. You are required only to bear half the cost of a standard fence. Make sure you put all the terms of your agreement in writing, and if the neighbour refuses to sign, you must obtain an order from the local court before commencing any work.

Fences and other construction work should never encroach on the property of an adjoining owner. Sometimes this occurs because of mistakes as to the location of the boundary. A surveyor's report should determine conclusively the position of the boundary in relation to buildings. Encroachments can be remedied by demolition in the case of inexpensive structures, but more serious encroachments may involve your neighbour granting you an easement for support or overhang, as the case may be (another good reason to be on favourable terms with your neighbour). If your neighbour is unwilling or unable to grant you the easement, you may have to purchase the parcel of land that supports your building from them. This is an expensive and complex business, and you would need proper advice.

Noise

Another problem that will often put a strain on good neighbourly relations is noise. Again, the best approach in the beginning is to talk to noisy neighbours on a friendly basis. Explain how they are disturbing your sleep or your dog or whatever else you have that is adversely affected by noise. If that fails, your next remedy is to approach the appropriate authority, and this will depend on the nature of the noise. Before you do this I would suggest a polite letter such as Letter 6.4. (See Letter 1.9 on page 20 if you need a stronger letter to an exceptionally difficult neighbour.)

6.4   Excessive noise letter

Mr Jack Hammer
186 Decibel Drive
CLAMOUR TOWN STA 22866

Dear Jack,

For the past few days you have been working in your garage with your hammer, banging away at your latest industrial project, and although I have mentioned the problems we are experiencing at our place as a result of the noise, still the hammering continues.

Slowly we are being driven to distraction. Last night you hammered until after midnight, completely ruining our night's sleep.

I would not normally write to you in these terms, particularly in view of our previous good relations, but the dog is off its food, the kids are staying over at friends, and Betty and I are too tired to get out of bed in the morning.

I intend to make a formal complaint to the police/local council/Pollution Control Commission unless the noise ceases immediately.

Yours sincerely,

Frank Neighbour

Whether to complain to the police, local council, or Pollution Control Commission will depend on the nature of the noise and the hours at which it is perpetrated. Generally, the authorities are most helpful, particularly the Pollution Control Commission, which has access to noise-measuring equipment that will determine the exact level of the noise. If the noise is recurring you may be entitled to an injunction to prevent it occurring in the future.

Negligence

An occupier of private property (whether a homeowner or tenant) has an obligation to guard against foreseeable injury to a person entering on the land or premises. In this sense everybody has a duty to protect visitors from injury, even if your neighbour illegally hops over the back fence. How a person comes onto your land is irrelevant to the question whether you owe a duty of care, although it may be a factor in assessing damages. A tenant may be responsible for defects in premises likely to cause injury even though the landlord is supposed to be looking after maintenance. Breach of the duty of care we owe to our neighbours is negligence. The way to guard against being sued for injuries to your neighbours on your property is to make sure your home and contents insurance cover includes public liability protection.

Many cases have been argued in the courts about injury to people on private premises. A common claim is for injury caused by tripping on worn carpet. It is a question of fact whether the carpet is worn and therefore inherently dangerous. If the carpet has become slippery or has holes that may cause a person to trip, a reasonable occupier will carry out repairs. Even if you warn your visitor about the carpet, you will still have an obligation to guard against the possibility that your visitor may forget about the danger. If you have an elderly visitor or a visitor with a disability, extra care is required to avoid exposing the visitor to any unusual risk.

A landlord is responsible for letting premises that are reasonably fit for use as a dwelling. Serious defects such as electrical faults that may cause injury and death to tenants need to be repaired. The landlord can delegate responsibility for inspecting the premises to a suitably qualified person. A wise landlord will arrange for a builder, electrician and plumber to inspect a house before introducing a tenant, otherwise they can be held responsible for protecting anyone who visits the tenant. Where the landlord has discharged their duty of care, it is the tenant who must guard against injury to neighbours.

A higher duty of care may exist where you invite large numbers of people to your home for a business meeting or party. Crowds tend to increase the risk of injury and you need to make sure your public liability insurance policy does not exclude the possibility of entertaining at home. Make sure you notify the insurance company if you work from home otherwise you may be in breach of the policy terms and conditions and the insurance company can deny your claim. If you have someone working for you at home such as domestic assistance, a child carer or gardener, you may need workers' compensation cover as well as public liability insurance. Apart from protecting the home worker from injury, you need to think about the possibility of injury to your neighbour caused by the negligence of your worker.

General complaints

Most disputes between neighbours can be resolved by talking. If you need a mediator your local Community Justice Centre has a free dispute resolution service. Mediation is the best solution for people with a continuing relationship such as neighbours. When mediation fails your local court will make a suitable determination provided you can prove the facts of your case. Again, before taking any action, the first thing you should do is talk to your neighbour. If the problem persists, write a nice letter. Letter 6.5 can be adapted to most neighbourhood disputes.

6.5   General complaint letter

Mr Joe Painful
21 Aggravation Drive
WARPVILLE STA 22411

Dear Joe,

For the past several weeks/months/days a problem has arisen in that [*state the problem in the fewest possible words*]. As you are aware, we have discussed the issues, and to date we do not appear to have resolved our differences.

While I am sympathetic to the views you have expressed, I feel that the continued [*again, state the problem using even fewer words than before*] will unfairly interfere with my privacy/damage my health/ endanger my safety/endanger my property.

I sincerely hope this letter will not cause any animosity between us, as we are destined to be neighbours for the foreseeable future, and in the past we have enjoyed good relations.

I will greatly appreciate any assistance you can give to help resolve the [*repeat the problem is one or two words*].

Yours sincerely,

A Houseproud

A. M. Houseproud (Ms)

A letter to your neighbour should be the last resort when all other lines of communication have been exhausted. Sometimes a simple letter that hits the spot can turn an otherwise sensible neighbour into a besieged lunatic. It is much better, therefore, to talk to your neighbour where possible instead of writing a letter.

Be prepared to make concessions. Most people do not want to fight with their neighbours and any compromises you make will generally be rewarded with good relations and often lasting friendships. Whatever happens, do not write an aggressive, threatening or challenging letter to your neighbour as you may set off a series of events that could ultimately put you to the expense and emotional upheaval of moving from the neighbourhood.

Chapter Seven

Car accidents

Motor vehicle damage claim

If you are involved in a motor vehicle accident and the accident is not your fault, you are entitled to recover from the person responsible for the accident the cost of repairing your vehicle. Provided you are fortunate enough to have insurance, you can make a claim on your comprehensive motor vehicle insurance policy and leave it to the insurance company to recover the repair costs. Where you need to make the claim yourself, write to the person responsible for the accident as soon as you obtain a quote for the cost of the repairs. Just to be on the safe side, obtain two repair quotes and ask the person to pay the cheaper of the two quotes. Letter 7.1 is a good place to start.

7.1   Letter claiming cost of repairs

Mr M. Benz
234 Reckless Highway
CARTOWN STA 21041

Dear Mr Benz,

I am the owner/driver of a motor vehicle registered number AWE-547 which was damaged in an accident with a motor vehicle registered number BAD-232 owned/driven by you on Morphetville Road, Cartown, on 15 June last. The accident was caused by your/your driver's negligence, and I have suffered loss of $800 as a result of the accident. I am enclosing two repair quotes and $800 is the cheaper of the two quotes.

I hope you will be in a position to compensate me for my loss and the purpose of this letter is to invite you to obtain a better quote for the repairs to my vehicle. If I do not hear from you within the next fourteen (14) days I will proceed to have the vehicle repaired and hold you responsible for the cost.

Assuming you are satisfied with the repair quote, please forward your cheque for $800 by return. Let me know if you need time to pay.

Yours sincerely,

Bill Damage

Bill Damage

The person responsible for the damage to your vehicle may be the driver or the owner of the other vehicle, or both. Generally, the driver will be regarded as the agent of the owner where they are not the same person. If you have any doubts about the ownership of the vehicle, check the records of your local traffic authority. Down the track you may need to sue and then you would join the owner and driver as defendants. In the circumstances where you are entitled to claim the cost of repairs on your own comprehensive insurance policy, you will still be out of pocket for the excess on the policy. Assuming you are seeking to recover only the policy excess, a friendly letter to the owner/driver of the vehicle that caused the damage to your vehicle may earn you a cheque in the mail. Try Letter 7.2 and hope for a co-operative defendant.

7.2 Letter claiming insurance excess

Mr M. Benz
234 Reckless Highway
CARTOWN STA 21041

Dear Mr Benz,

I am the owner of a motor vehicle registered number AWE-547 which was damaged in an accident with a motor vehicle registered number BAD-232 owned/driven by you on Morphetville Road, Cartown, on 15 June last. The accident was caused by your/your driver's negligence, and I have suffered loss of $400 being the amount of the excess on my insurance policy.

I am enclosing a copy of a letter from my insurance company confirming the excess and I look forward to receiving your cheque for $400 at your convenience.

Yours sincerely,

Bill Damage

Bill Damage

It is most important not to have your vehicle repaired until the person responsible for the accident has had the opportunity to obtain an alternative repair quotation. They may know somebody in the business who can do a good job at a reasonable price. If you are making a claim on your own insurance company, you can be sure the company will want to inspect the damage before admitting your claim. The company will advise you when the repairs can be carried out. If there is a dispute with the motor vehicle repairer as to the cost of repairs or standard of the repair work, most States and Territories have a Motor Vehicle Repair Disputes Committee to help resolve the problem.

Often your initial letter of demand will fail to get a response and then you should send a stronger follow-up letter. Letter 7.3 may be useful.

7.3 Follow-up letter

Mr M. Benz
234 Reckless Highway
CARTOWN STA 21041

Dear Mr Benz,

I refer to my previous letter to you requesting your cheque for $800/$400 to compensate me for my loss in the accident at Morphetville Road, Cartown, on 15 June last.

To date I have not received your cheque, and unless some arrangement is made to pay the amount due within twenty-one (21) days, I intend commencing court proceedings without further notice.

Yours faithfully,

Bill Damage

Bill Damage

If proceedings become necessary, check the records of your local traffic authority to find out the owner of the vehicle before filing your claim, otherwise you could sue the wrong person. Where the driver is a different person from the owner, you should name both as defendants in the proceedings. You can run the claim yourself in the local court provided liability is not in question. Seek advice before commencing proceedings if the defendant disputes your claim. At the hearing of the claim you will not be entitled to raise matters not included in the summons, so your pleadings should include all possible causes of action.

Defending a claim

Where you are on the receiving end of a claim for damage to another vehicle, and you believe the accident was not your fault, you are entitled to dispute the claim. Letter 7.4 is a suitable letter to the person claiming the cost of repairs.

7.4   Reply to demand

Mr Bill Damage
121 Contributory Way
CARTOWN STA 21041

Dear Mr Damage,

I refer to your recent letter requesting payment of $800/$400 for repairs to/insurance excess on your vehicle registered number AWE-547 which was damaged in an accident on Morphetville Road, Cartown, on 15 June last.

The purpose of this letter is to inform you that I dispute your claim as you were wholly/partly responsible for the accident. In any event, the amount of your claim is excessive, and I would be obliged if you could make your vehicle available to John Smith Smash Repairs of Cartown for an independent assessment of the damage.

Yours faithfully,

M. Benz

M. Benz (Mr)

In a situation where the person or their insurance company making the claim commences proceedings, you are entitled to defend the proceedings and make a cross-claim for the damage to your vehicle. If you are insured, pass the summons on to your insurance company, and let them worry about it. If not, get advice from a suitably qualified lawyer who will tell you the issues you need to raise and how to include them in your defence and cross-claim. As I said a moment ago, any issue you intend raising at the hearing must be included in the pleadings, otherwise you will be precluded from arguing that issue.

Your local court will reach a decision based on the percentage of responsibility each person bears for the accident. If you are 80 per cent responsible, you pay 80 per cent of the damage to both vehicles. Because the proceedings are conducted in a civil court, the civil onus of proof applies, and the court will make its determination according to the balance of probabilities. You may be a bit short on evidence that the other party was twenty per cent responsible for the accident, but provided you can hold together the thread of an argument, usually the court will be sympathetic if your case is reasonable. In the motor vehicle damages business few stories are novel, whether on the police record or the insurance company files, and some unlikely explanations often get a run.

Involving the police

You must notify the police about a car accident where somebody is injured or substantial damage has been caused to one or both

vehicles. Once, I ran into a truck, causing no damage to the truck, but my car was too badly damaged to drive. The truck driver gave me details of his name and address plus the name and address of the owner of the truck. A tow truck happened to be passing (as they do) and the driver stopped and gave me some good advice. Although I had an obligation to notify the police about the accident (usually within 24 hours), no purpose would be served by calling them to the scene, according to the tow truck driver, as I would almost certainly be charged with a traffic offence—perhaps negligent driving. Under the law at that time the advice was quite correct and no obligation existed to call the police.

The tow truck driver towed my car to the nearest police station where I filled out an Accident Report form. I invited the desk constable to inspect the car to confirm that the accident was my fault. The tow truck driver rolled his eyes and the police officer said, 'Sign here'. To this day I have not heard a word from the police about the accident. As I mentioned earlier, you should not make admissions about liability in a car accident as you might compromise your insurance policy. Another reason for silence about the question of fault is the possibility of police charges. Since this particular incident, a change to the law in New South Wales now means you are obliged to call the police to an accident where a vehicle needs to be towed away.

Other circumstances in which police must be called to the scene of an accident include the difficult situation where a driver will not provide details of their name, address and licence number; a driver fails to stop or leaves the accident scene without providing details; a driver appears to be under the influence of alcohol or other drugs; damage is caused to property other than the vehicles involved in the accident; or somebody has injuries that require medical treatment. You must assist an injured person to the best of your ability and this would include dialing 000 for an ambulance. Another problem at the scene of an accident is the potential hazard caused by other motorists and you should take whatever steps are necessary to warn approaching drivers to slow down.

Where you are responsible for the accident and the only damage is to the vehicles involved, the police may issue a traffic fine on the spot. Alternatively, you will receive a fine in the post after the details of the accident have been processed by police administration. It is not uncommon for the police to allege multiple breaches of the traffic laws based on information obtained at the scene of an accident. After the event, however, you may have second thoughts about the circumstances of the accident, or something that was said at the scene may be troubling you. A question might arise, for example, about the condition of the road, or whether a witness gave police a fair report of what happened.

If you feel aggrieved by police charges when the whole circumstances of an accident are pretty grey, you should canvass the issues with your local police commissioner. Before doing this you may want to obtain a copy of the police accident report. You will be charged a small fee (check with the accident information unit at the Police Department), but the police accident report will allow you to assess the accident through the eyes of the police. You may find that the police have an angle you did not consider. On the other hand, the police may have missed something, prompting you to write to the commissioner. Make sure you write well before the return date on the summons and as soon as possible in any event. If the police accident report is delayed, write on a 'Without Prejudice' basis. Letter 7.5 may assist you.

7.5   Letter to police

WITHOUT PREJUDICE

Mr Ace Bluey
Commissioner of Police
142 Traffic Boulevarde
CARTOWN STA 21041

Dear Mr Bluey,

I refer to the traffic fine handed to me by Constable Bloggs of Upbeat Police Station on 15 June last following an accident on Morphetville Road, Cartown. You may not be aware that the following events occurred in the moments leading up to the accident.

- A cat ran across the path of my vehicle as I was travelling in an easterly direction along Morphetville Road.
- I swerved to the incorrect side of the road to avoid the cat and was confronted by a horse. I am allergic to horses and sneezed.
- When I opened my eyes the horse had leapt out of the path of my vehicle, thereby exposing me to another vehicle travelling in the opposite direction.

I would be grateful if you could take the above matters into consideration and perhaps you will see your way clear to cancelling the traffic fine.

Yours sincerely,

Royce

R. Royce (Mr)

If you seriously challenge the traffic fine and intend to dispute it, a copy of your letter can be tendered in evidence at the hearing. A summons will issue as a matter of course following non-payment of the fine. As government departments go, the police service is a rarity in that you can get action by doing nothing. By the same token, the police are more sympathetic than you might think. A few years ago I represented a motorist who was responsible for the death of a person in a motor vehicle accident. The motorist was summonsed for an extremely serious traffic offence carrying a gaol term. I wrote to the police commissioner suggesting that the circumstances of the accident warranted a lesser charge, particularly as the deceased was partly responsible for the accident. The commissioner agreed and the original charge was withdrawn.

On another occasion I advised a motorist who wrote to the commissioner of police, several government ministers, the traffic authority and the local council after he received a fine for negligent driving. By the time the file was passed around from one authority to the next, the period in which a summons must issue had elapsed—usually six months. The time and patience required for such an enterprise, however, would rarely be justified, and your energies would be better directed to preparing a defence when the case goes to court.

Involving the court

Often it will not be convenient to go to court to answer a police charge for a minor breach of the traffic regulations. You are entitled to an adjournment, but you may prefer to have the matter disposed of, particularly if there is little doubt you were at fault. In such a case it would be appropriate to write to the court and ask that certain mitigating factors be taken into account on the question of penalty. Try Letter 7.6 as a starting point.

7.6   Letter to court

Mr S. M. Beak
Presiding Magistrate
Justice Town Traffic Court
97 Bench Boulevard
JUSTICE TOWN STA 29777

Dear Mr Beak,

I am listed to appear before the court on 15 October next, on a charge of negligent driving following an accident on Morphetville Road, Cartown, on 15 June last. Due to pressing family/employment commitments, it will not be possible for me to attend court on that day, and I would like to see the case dealt with as soon as possible.

I request that you hear the charge against me in my absence, and on the question of penalty, I ask that the following matters be taken into account:

1. I have been driving for fifteen years and in that time I have had only three previous fines for breaches of the traffic regulations.
2. I am a member of the Cartown Community Services Club and generally a person of good character.
3. I am usually a careful driver and would not normally drive on the incorrect side of the road in the circumstances noted by the police.

Prevailing economic conditions are such that a heavy fine would cause me severe financial hardship.

I hope you will see your way clear to giving my case your favourable consideration.

Yours sincerely,

R. Royce

R. Royce (Mr)

Nothing is to be gained from telling the court about the cat running across the road or your allergy to horses. These things are already on file, assuming you raised them with the police officer when you were booked, and the appropriate course if you want to press them is to attend court and plead not guilty to the charge of negligent driving. Unless you are prepared to appear personally to defend yourself, the court has no alternative but to accept the police evidence and find you guilty. You must attend court personally for more serious traffic infringements, particularly where somebody has been injured in the accident.

Motor vehicle accident injuries

On the question of compensation if you are injured in a motor vehicle accident, the amount of compensation will depend on the extent of your injuries, loss of past and future income as a result of the accident, nursing and domestic care if you need it, and rehabilitation and medical expenses. If your injuries are in the top ten per cent of the worst injuries category, you will also receive compensation for pain and suffering and the loss of enjoyment of your life caused by the accident. This is called general damages. The compensation will be paid by compulsory third party insurance, or, where the person responsible for the accident is not insured or not identified, by a statutory body called the Nominal Defendant.

You may be surprised to learn that while people who are seriously injured in motor vehicle accidents often receive large compensation payouts, the amount paid to the relatives of someone who is killed (where the deceased person had no dependants) may be limited to the cost of the funeral and a headstone. The reason for this apparent injustice is that the common law looks at the question of economic loss—the amount of money an injured person has lost in earning capacity as a result of the accident. A deceased person has no earning capacity, according to the common law, and therefore no compensation is payable to the person's relatives for future loss of income.

Another apparent anomaly in compensation laws for injuries received in a motor vehicle accident relates to the question of fault. You must prove that the accident was the fault of somebody other than yourself. Regrettably, if you were at fault you will not receive any compensation for your injuries, even if they are horrendous. Most cases will involve proving the person responsible for the accident was negligent. In other words, you must prove the person owed you a duty of care, he or she breached that duty of care and as a result you suffered loss or damage. Some examples of a breach of the duty of care include driving too fast, failing to keep a proper lookout, driving on the incorrect side of the road and driving while affected by alcohol or other drugs.

Provided the third party insurance company of the person responsible for the accident admits liability, the claim is relatively straightforward, particularly in those States and Territories where a Motor Accidents Authority (MAA) has been established. The MAA is run by the State or Territory government and is virtually a one-stop-shop for people injured in motor vehicle accidents where the third party insurer admits liability. Insurers are accountable to the MAA both in respect of profitability and payments on claims. Everything is dealt with by the MAA from filling out the claim form to assessing your injuries. If you have been injured in a motor vehicle accident, Letter 7.7 to the MAA is a good place to start on the road to recovery.

7.7   Letter to the MAA

Ms Mary Bloggs
Claims Manager
Motor Accidents Authority
Level 22, 580 George Street
SYDNEY NSW 2000

Dear Ms Bloggs,

I was injured in a motor vehicle accident on 31 January last and I would like some re-assurance about my treatment and rehabilitation. I have been unable to work since the accident and I cannot afford medical expenses.

The person responsible for the accident informed me he cannot recall the name of his third party insurer. His name is John Smith and he drives a Toyota Corolla registered number BAD-111. Please let me know the name of his insurance company and whether the company admits liability.

I reported the accident to Constable Jones of Morphetville Police Station. Constable Jones attended the scene of the accident, but I was too distressed to sign an accident report form. I will be happy to do so as soon as I am well enough if you think it is necessary. Please let me know about my obligations.

At this stage I am unable to attend your office to sign the relevant claim form. In the meantime you might be kind enough to forward me the form and let me know what I am to do about the medical expenses.

Yours sincerely,

A. Victim

A. Victim (Ms)

You must make your claim for personal injury compensation within six months of the accident. If the MAA will not accept your claim because of a disputed question of liability, you can obtain legal advice about the possibility of court proceedings. Any proceedings must be commenced within three years of the accident. Where you are partly responsible for the accident the MAA will still process your claim on the basis that your compensation will be discounted by a percentage equivalent to your contribution to the accident. You will be partly at fault if, for example, you were not wearing a seatbelt, you were driving at an unsafe speed, you travelled with a driver you knew was affected by alcohol or other drugs, or you drove yourself while under the influence of drugs or alcohol.

The MAA produces a number of excellent brochures and they are available from your doctor or lawyer. You will notice that the brochures focus on rehabilitation and recovery rather than promoting confrontation and litigation. One of the objectives of the MAA is to make insurance companies more accountable both for their profits and the way they process claims for motor accident injuries. It is intended that the authority will literally hold the hand of people injured in motor accidents. More will be said about this new system for dealing with the insurance industry in the next section on insurance claim letters.

Chapter Eight

Insurance claims

Making a claim

Look around the skylines of the world's major cities and you will find insurance companies well represented in the glass and concrete towers that symbolise the postwar economic miracle. Insurance companies and banks dominate the naming rights on these edifices to free enterprise—or modern towers of Babel reaching for an inappropriate heaven, depending on your view of how the world goes around. Like banking, insurance is big business, but with none of the safety nets and social aspirations of the major banks. While the Commonwealth Bank paid nearly $1 billion in tax last year, many insurance companies appeared to be in the red, and at the time of writing, problems with insurance companies appear in newspaper headlines and occupy our political and civil agendas in a way that is completely out of proportion to their importance.

Insurance is a middle class comfort to help us feel secure about our material possessions. Neither the rich (including the government) nor the poor bother with insurance, leaving the middle class to bear its own burdens when insurance companies fail to meet their financial obligations. Recently, a receiver was appointed to manage the affairs of HIH Insurance Company,

Australia's second-largest insurer, leaving two million people up the proverbial creek so far as their insurance was concerned. Many professional groups such as lawyers are currently operating without professional indemnity insurance despite statutory obligations to insure themselves against negligence. Thousands of private citizens have outstanding claims involving their homes and personal effects with no prospect of recovery without government intervention. Serious questions need to be answered about the role of government watchdogs in the HIH collapse.

All insurance companies work on the principle that the premiums they receive exceed the amount of claims. The biggest risk in taking out an insurance policy is that the company will happily take your premium and then be unable or unwilling to pay your claim. And the more you claim, the more your premiums will increase. Motor vehicle insurance, for instance, provides for a 'no claim bonus' which is reflected in your premium for each year you do not make a claim up to a maximum of 60 per cent of the scheduled premium. The less drain you are on the insurance company the less drain they are on you.

In deciding whether or not you will make a claim, the real question is whether the increased premium you will pay as a result of the claim exceeds the value of the claim. If you make an insurance claim on your motor vehicle policy, for example, for an amount of $800, and your premium increases from $400 to $800 as a result of the claim, then it is hardly worth the effort of filling out the claim form. If you do decide to claim, Letter 8.1 is a reasonable letter to the insurance company to be forwarded with the claim form.

8.1 General claim letter

Mr N. O. Cover
Claims Manager
Obstacle Insurance Company
44 Marathon Road
HURDLE PARK STA 28444

Dear Mr Cover,

Enclosed please find claim form duly completed for loss under policy number 12345. The amount of the claim is $800 and I trust you will undertake appropriate investigations and process the claim without delay.

You will notice from the claim form that the loss was not due to any carelessness or fault on my part and consequently I hope you will not increase my insurance premium as a consequence of the claim. I look forward to your advice in that regard.

Please acknowledge my claim and confirm you admit liability for the loss.

Yours sincerely,

V. Hopeful

V. Hopeful (Ms)

Lodge your claim as soon as possible after you have suffered the loss or damage as many insurance policies have time limits in which to lodge claims. If the loss or damage is not your fault, you should tell the insurance company and put it on notice that you trust it will not increase your premiums as a result of the claim. And there is always the remote possibility that the insurance company will value your business sufficiently to do the right thing.

Changing insurance companies

Should the insurance company increase your premium in spite of the letter, or before you have the opportunity to write a letter, the next thing to do is to shop around and find a company that will give you a cheaper premium. Make sure the company is reputable, although it needs to be said that HIH Insurance Company had a good reputation before it went bust. Perhaps you need to get advice from an accountant or lawyer before deciding whether cheap premiums also mean a poor claims record.

Once you have found a new insurer you will want to write to the old company and vent your spleen. Before you express the way you feel, however, make sure your new insurer has actually written a cover note or policy. Burning your insurance bridges before alternative arrangements are in place could leave you without appropriate cover. Letter 8.2 is a suitable farewell to the old company.

8.2   Letter rejecting increased premium

Mr N. O. Cover
Claims Manager
Obstacle Insurance Company
44 Marathon Road
HURDLE PARK STA 28444

Dear Mr Cover,

I refer to your recent account suggesting my insurance premium in respect of policy number 12345 will increase from $250 to $400 for the current year.

Although I appreciate the importance to your organisation of making a large profit, I regret that I am not in a position to assist you in this endeavour at the present time.

It is my intention, therefore, to obtain cover from another insurance company in a smaller building than the one occupied by your company, or not to continue my cover.

Should you decide to reduce your profit or move to a smaller building at any time in the future, then I will be pleased to consider your new premiums.

Yours faithfully,

V. Hopeful

V. Hopeful (Ms)

In expressing the way you feel about insurance companies, it is worth recalling that some insurances are compulsory. For instance, if you have a motor vehicle under lease or hire purchase agreement, it will be a condition of the contract that you keep the vehicle insured. Doctors, lawyers, financial advisers, accountants, surveyors, valuers and numerous other professionals all carry professional indemnity policies. Also, if you are an employer you will be required to keep employees covered for workers' compensation insurance.

Workers' compensation insurance

On average in any one year in Australia 2500 people will die due to their work, 15 000 workers will be permanently incapacitated or away from work for three months and 300 000 claims for workers' compensation will be successful. The human cost of work is staggering and the financial cost to employers no less incredible. Average workers' compensation insurance premiums in New South Wales amount to 2.8 per cent of gross wages and the statutory authority, WorkCover, is said to have a deficit of

$2 billion. At the time of writing the government is trying to push through legislation to reduce the deficit by cutting workers' benefits, particularly common law payments and legal fees, which between them represent about 25 per cent of workers' compensation payouts. Common law benefits are payable where an employer is negligent and it is generally agreed that a worker will receive higher payments at common law than under the WorkCover statutory compensation scheme.

If you are an employer it is wise to avoid speculation about the cause of a workplace accident. Do not get caught up in rumours about who or what was involved. Limit your report to what you could see with your own eyes and what you heard with your own ears. Otherwise you may unwittingly compromise yourself under the terms of your workers' compensation insurance policy, or you may prejudice your employee in subsequent workers' compensation proceedings. When an employee has left work as a result of an accident or illness, you should immediately notify the insurance company, and leave the financial and medical decisions about the employee to the statutory authority. WorkCover will give you guidance about finding a person to replace the injured employee and your obligations to provide light duties when the employee is fit to resume work. Use Letter 8.3 to notify the insurance company of the claim.

8.3   Letter to insurance company

Mr D. Bosca
General Manager
Everyworkers Insurance Company
126 Accident Way
WORKINGTOWN STA 22440

Dear Mr Bosca,

We are the holders of policy number 27429 and we hereby give you notice of an intended claim for compensation by our employee,

John Smith, who was injured in an accident on 25 March last. A completed claim form and supporting statements are enclosed.

Yours sincerely,
Australian Industrial Company

V Responsible

V. Responsible (Mr)
Personnel Manager

Workers' compensation is in reality a pension scheme—and not a good one by any standard. Weekly payments after six months are less than the dole, and lump sum payments either at common law or under the statutory scheme are never sufficient to compensate an injured worker for the loss of their job or the grief of being injured at work. The idea that workers routinely rort the workers' compensation system has no basis in fact. Nobody who works in the workers' compensation industry believes this myth whether they are workers or employers. Nevertheless, some workers experience a sense of guilt about workplace injuries and often they will benefit from a letter of support from a sympathetic employer. Letter 8.4 may do the job.

8.4 Letter to employee

Mr Abel Yakka
220 Recovery Way
WORKINGTOWN STA 22440

Dear Abel,

We sincerely regret your workplace injury and wish you a speedy recovery. You are one of our key people and we wonder how we will get by without you.

Temporary measures are in place to fill your position, but we want to emphasise that your position will be available as soon as you have recovered. We look forward to seeing you back at work when you are fit for light duties.

In the meantime you should get as much rest as possible and make the most of the time with your family.

Yours sincerely,
Australian Industrial Company

V. Responsible

V. Responsible (Mr)
Personnel Manager

Another myth that needs to be exploded about workers' compensation is that workers are somehow responsible for negligent employers and therefore access to common law damages should be restricted. Any cap or other limitation on a worker's full entitlements is both unfair and onerous according to the New South Wales Bar Association. Statutory compensation schemes for injured workers (and injured motorists, for that matter) do have a price, however. In practice, only about one per cent of injured workers (and ten per cent of injured motorists) have access to full common law damages. Any further attempts, therefore, to limit the rights of workers who are injured because of their employers' negligence ought to be restricted. At the time of writing the Labor government in New South Wales and the union movement are bitterly divided on proposals to further reduce the rights of workers to sue for injuries caused by negligent employers.

One of the difficulties for employers when an injured employee returns to work is that the employer cannot be certain that the employee is fit to do the job. The employer is anxious not to aggravate the employee's injury, but at the same time the employer will want the job completed in an efficient manner. Often the insurance company will have up-to-date medical reports as to the condition of the employee, but the employer (and the employee) will not be so privileged. In those circumstances it is not unreasonable for the employer to request a medical report from the medical practitioner most familiar with the condition of the employee. Letter 8.5 is a good precedent.

8.5 Letter to doctor

Dr W. Comp
231 Recovery Way
WORKINGTOWN STA 22440

Dear Dr Comp,

We are the employers of John Smith who was injured in a workplace accident on 25 March last. Mr Smith is anxious to resume work and we would be obliged if you could supply us with a medical report as to his condition, stating particularly:

1. The nature and extent of his injury/illness.
2. His present disability, if any.
3. His future disability, if any.
4. The type of work he is fit to undertake.

An authority for the report signed by Mr Smith is enclosed.

We look forward to receiving the report and we undertake to attend to payment of your fees in connection with the report as soon as your account is received.

Yours sincerely,
Australian Industrial Company

V. Responsible

V. Responsible (Mr)
Personnel Manager

Health insurance

If you decide to take out private health insurance cover with one of the health funds, you will be entitled to treatment as a private patient in a public or private hospital. You will also be covered for some expenses not covered by Medicare. Recently, I took out private cover in response to an advertising campaign by the federal government to the effect that if I take out the cover now I will always pay the same premium. It cannot be true, of course, but government propaganda is so misleading these days (think about the GST) that people simply learn to live with the untruths. In any case, I had been on a waiting list for non-urgent surgery for more than three years, and private cover seemed like a good way to jump the queue, even allowing for the twelve months' waiting period before I could claim.

The burning issue in private health insurance at present is 'gap cover'—that is, the diffference between the cost of treatment and the amount you can expect your insurer to reimburse you. It appears that 50 per cent of medical specialists charge a fee of less than $200 above the Commonwealth Medicare Benefits Schedule, and if you have 'gap cover' insurance you can expect the insurer to pay this additional fee. If your medical specialist charges in excess of the gap cover fee then the insurer will pay only the schedule fee. In such a case the specialist will bill you direct for the total cost of your care and they must provide you with a written quote, including a written estimate of out-of-pocket expenses, before you receive treatment. You must acknowledge the quote and I suggest Letter 8.6 is a good response to the specialist.

8.6 Letter to medical specialist

Dr Tony Bloggs
Vascular Surgeon
St Vincent's Clinic
Victoria Street
DARLINGHURST NSW 2010

Dear Dr Bloggs,

Thank you for your itemised estimate of the cost of my medical procedure. I acknowledge the total cost at $3670 calculated as follows:

Hospital accommodation fee	
(three days at $380 per day)	1140.00
Anaesthetist	790.00
Theatre fee	340.00
Sutures, bandages, etc.	80.00
Your fee for the operation	900.00
Post-operative consultations	420.00
	3670.00

I accept the estimate and I note that it does not include additional fees and out-of-pocket expenses that may be necessary in an emergency. Needless to say, I hope an emergency will not arise, but if it does you are authorised to take whatever steps are reasonably necessary to look after my health.

Yours sincerely,

A Bitcrook

A. Bitcrook (Ms)

Rules vary between health funds, but generally they will pay the account where the specialist is onboard with the gap cover arrangements. Otherwise you must pay the account yourself and seek reimbursement from the insurer. Most hospitals will do the paperwork for you and you would simply pay the hospital the difference between the schedule fee and the amount your specialist has charged. The hospital would then seek reimbursement of the schedule fee from Medicare (75 per cent) and the health fund (25 per cent).

Superannuation insurance

Employers in Australia are required to pay superannuation for employees. At present the rate is seven per cent of the employee's annual salary, rising to nine per cent in 2002. Superannuation savings are intended to reduce future demands on the government for the age pension. Successive federal governments have assured us that the age pension will continue at around 25 per cent of average weekly earnings, but with an ageing population and inequities in the superannuation industry, you need to make decisions about your retirement arrangements almost in spite of the government. Many people who run small businesses, for example, consider superannuation as a luxury they cannot afford.

Another aspect of superannuation that deters people in small business is the high administration costs charged by the fund managers. In my opinion, you are better off buying shares or investment property than paying superannuation fund managers to lead the high life. This is a reasonable argument from the point of view of a person in a small business since you lose about two per cent of your superannuation contributions in administration expenses when you pay into a large fund. Control is also an important consideration for many people. Why trust the fund managers when the investment record of successful small business operators speaks for itself?

Some people run their own superannuation funds with the assistance of an accountant or lawyer with expertise in the area. Small companies often set up their own funds and provide employee benefits which often exceed the compulsory scheme benefits. Industry funds are also popular, particularly for professional bodies and large industry groups such as retailers and builders. Contributions are set by industrial awards and the fund is managed by an industry trust. Public sector funds are run by State and Territory governments under an agreement with the Commonwealth. With the exception of the captains of industry and politicians, few people have the opportunity to make adequate provision for their retirement. Superannuation creates large companies and tall buildings, but generally fails to provide financial security for the people contributing the money.

Chapter Nine

Debtors and creditors

Debtors seeking extended credit

Management of creditors is a business skill that requires self-restraint because easy credit can get you into as much trouble as insufficient capital. I once knew a home builder who extended his credit from 30 days to 60 days and built two extra houses each month with the extra cash the exercise put in his business. For all his ingenuity, the builder eventually went broke when he needed 90 days' credit about the same time the creditors needed their money. You should extend a creditor only if you have a sound business—in case your own credit is withdrawn on short notice—and only with the approval of the creditor. Try Letter 9.1 as a starting point.

9.1 Letter requesting extended credit

Mr Jarrah Woodstock
General Manager
Creditline Timber Company
145 Forest Way
TREE VALLEY STA 23121

Dear Jarrah,

For the past several years we have relied on your company as the major source of timber for our range of homes and in that time we have always paid our accounts promptly and within the period of 30 days as provided by our credit arrangements.

Because of the recent expansion of our home building operation and an increase in our timber requirements, we find that an extension of our credit facility is desirable in order to meet the increased demand for our product.

We believe our timber order will expand to something in the vicinity of 200 cubic metres per month and in those circumstances we consider an extension of our credit facility to 60 days would be reasonable.

Kindly give the above request your favourable consideration.

Yours sincerely,
Growth Homes Corporation

O. P. Timistic

O. P. Timistic (Mr)
General Manager

This letter is offering something in return for an extended credit facility, namely, a larger order, and it is fundamental to any request for credit to offer something in return. Under no circumstances should you ask for credit because you have no money. Your trading partners will become nervous and may withdraw the credit you have. By all means indicate why you want the credit, but 'to meet the increased demand on our resources' is as close as you would want to come to saying you need a quid. You may prefer to use the words 'to assist in our expansion program'. From the creditor's point of view, however, it is a bit rich to be asked to fund the expansion program of somebody who owes you money.

Most businesses experience periods of difficult trading. Creditors will generally extend credit in these periods, but it is important to keep creditors informed of your trading activities. It takes only one disgruntled creditor to call a creditors' meeting and ultimately wind up your business operation. If you have a creditor you cannot satisfy for the time being and you know he or she is taking steps to stop you trading, you can forestall that creditor by communicating with other creditors to satisfy them you are in a position to trade out of your difficulties. Adapt Letter 9.2 for this purpose.

9.2 Letter confirming solvency

Mr Jarrah Woodstock
General Manager
Creditline Timber Company
145 Forest Way
TREE VALLEY STA 23121

Dear Jarrah,

You may be aware that steps have been taken by Blockage Plumbing Services to appoint a receiver to our home building operation in the belief that we are unable to trade out of our present difficulties. The purpose of this letter is to inform you we have restructured our affairs to reduce overheads and increase profit. We enclose a copy of the following documents prepared by our accountants:

- profit and loss statement;
- balance sheet; and
- projected cash flow statement.

You will notice in particular that several assets are listed for sale and others have already been sold. Previously unprofitable activities have been terminated.

We ask that you allow us the opportunity to continue trading and accept our assurance that the profit projected in the cash flow statement will be achieved.

Our cheque for $1800 being that part of your account outstanding for a period in excess of 30/60 days, is enclosed.

Yours sincerely,
Growth Homes Corporation

O. P. Timistic

O. P. Timistic (Mr)
General Manager

You may not be in a position to pay anything, in which case you simply leave out the last paragraph. No more convincing way exists to satisfy creditors, however, than to make an effort to bring your payments up to date. Another option is to reach an informal arrangement with your creditors to pay what you can afford by instalments. If things are really tough you may want to consider a formal debt arrangement under Part X of the Bankruptcy Act. In this case you would need to contact a solicitor or registered trustee to call a meeting of your creditors.

Negotiating with a creditor

Sometimes a creditor will press for payment and even attempt to wind you up (in the legal sense) when a genuine dispute exists with the creditor as to the amount or validity of the claim. An unscrupulous creditor might communicate with other creditors in the hope that the collective pressure will force you to give up or compromise your dispute. One of the good things about repressive defamation laws is that the law protects us from a creditor seeking to shortcut a dispute. You should send Letter 9.3 to such a creditor.

9.3   Letter to an unreasonable creditor

Mr U. Creditor
General Secretary
Pressure Sales & Service
222 Foxy Way
DISPUTED TERRITORY STA 23240

Dear Mr Creditor,

I refer to your claim for payment of $1200 for the supply of 100 dozen plastic washers. As you are aware, I dispute your claim in that the washers supplied were not suitable for their intended purpose as outlined in my original order and accompanying specification.

It has been brought to my attention that you have communicated with my trade suppliers with a view to appointing a receiver of my business. Such action by you is a total outrage and completely ignores the fact that I dispute your claim. May I remind you of the defamation laws and inform you that your action has seriously affected my reputation and the longstanding credit arrangements I have with suppliers.

As to your alleged claim, appropriate remedies are available to you if you believe the claim is justified, but such remedies do not include damaging my business or personal reputation, and any further defamatory statements will result in legal action.

Yours sincerely,
Metal Manufacturing Company

Steele Nerve
General Manager

A vast number of small businesses fail in the first two or three years after they are set up, but once you are established, creditors in general do not want to put you out of business. You are probably a valued customer and most creditors will be aware that business has its ups and downs. If your credit is fully extended or you are inclined or obliged to reduce your business activities, it may be desirable to explain your difficulties to your creditors and seek time to pay. When your debts are paid you will be much more popular with your creditors than somebody else who has extended too far and been wound up. Creditors will generally receive only a fraction of their debt from the liquidator or receiver if you are declared insolvent. Letter 9.4 is a letter to a creditor requesting time to pay.

9.4 Letter requesting time to pay

Ms V. Compassionate
Accounts Manager
Credit Flour Supply Company
127 Instalment Street
CROSSROADS STA 26122

Dear Ms Compassionate,

For the past several months/years you have been supplying me with flour for my cake shop at Narrow Street, Crossroads. You have been kind enough to provide me with credit, which has greatly assisted me to operate the business.

You will be aware that my account is presently in arrears and that the amount due exceeds our normal credit arrangements. I regret that this situation has occurred, but I am experiencing unusual/serious trading difficulties at the present time, and the purpose of this letter is to seek time to pay the amount due.

I expect I will be in a position to pay you the sum of $200 per month commencing at the end of this month until the debt is paid.

Please indicate your requirements at the earliest opportunity and I hope you will be in a position to accede to my request.

Yours sincerely,
Crossroads Cake Shop

Sue Dough.

Sue Dough
General Manager

Whether you tell your supplier you are experiencing 'unusual' or 'serious' trading difficulties will depend on whether or not you intend staying in business. Obviously, 'serious' means some doubt exists about your solvency, and if you say 'serious' when you mean 'unusual', you may find your creditor is not too receptive. Apart from anything else the creditor might do, they could stop your supply of flour, and that would be a disaster if you intend to continue trading. You will notice also that this letter does not inform the creditor what you intend doing to improve your trading position. It is not the kind of information you would volunteer unless you are in desperate straits and trying to convince your creditor about your solvency.

If you already have a loan and you are struggling to meet the repayments, you may be entitled to have the contract reviewed under consumer credit laws. You could have the repayments reduced and the term of the loan extended, provided you can demonstrate hardship. Some cases of hardship include unemployment, illness, family breakdown and unexpected expense such as a car accident. It is up to you to make the application to your creditor before they take action against you under the loan contract. Sometimes creditors are only interested in receiving the scheduled loan repayments. If this is the case, you should get help from your local Consumer Affairs Department. If your creditor is a bank or financial institution you will need to provide as much information as possible to secure reduced loan repayments. Letter 9.5 may be helpful.

9.5   Letter seeking variation of repayments

Mr Don Satrap
Lending Manager
Usury Bank
44 Railway Road
CAPITAL CORNER STA 24444

Dear Mr Satrap,

You will be aware that my loan repayments are one month behind and the purpose of this letter is to request a review of the loan. Since taking out the loan I have experienced a change of circumstances in that [*state the reasons you are unable to maintain your loan repayments*].

I am hoping you will accept reduced repayments until my circumstances improve. The most I can afford at the present time is [*state the amount*] based on my [*reduced income/increased commitments*]. Supporting documents confirming my changed circumstances are enclosed.

I do not expect any improvement in my situation until [*set out expected date*] and I would then propose resuming my scheduled repayments. Alternatively, you may agree to reduced repayments and extending the term of the loan. I understand this is an option under the credit laws in cases of financial hardship.

As I indicated to you on the telephone, I sincerely regret that the problem with [*repeat in two or three words the reason you need to review your repayments*] has arisen and I fully expect to be back on my feet within the time contemplated. I will be guided by you as to the appropriate adjustment to the amount and term of my loan repayments.

Yours sincerely,

N. O. Mooney

N. O. Money (Ms)

Creditors as letter writers

Creditors are noted for the brevity of their correspondence if they bother to write at all. It is wise to write as a creditor, however, in order to keep track of who owes you money. For one thing, the amount of unpaid debts people in business carry is staggering. The figure for most businesses runs between ten and twenty per cent of turnover. Unpaid debts can easily get out

of hand, and more and more people are insisting on cash up front, particularly in service industries. Unfortunately for manufacturing industries, customers rarely pay in advance as they want to see what they are getting before they part with their hard-earned cash. Nevertheless, manufacturers are also tending to require deposits with orders and cash on delivery. If you are owed money and you are not prepared to extend a debtor's credit any further, write Letter 9.6 to the debtor.

9.6 Letter of demand

Mr O. D. Account
452 Credit Place
DEBTORS VALLEY STA 26477

Dear Mr Account,

We refer to previous requests for payment of our outstanding account for the sum of $1200. We have received no response to our requests, and you have failed to make satisfactory arrangements for payment of the amount due.

We regret that we are not in a position to carry the debt any longer and legal action will be commenced immediately for recovery of the amount due plus costs without further notice.

Yours faithfully,
Business Afloat Corporation

A M Buoyant

A. M. Buoyant (Ms)
Accounts Manager

The letter of demand has a good track record because the first paragraph indicates to the debtor that they have the option to pay the amount due by instalments. From the debtor's point of view, an arrangement to pay by instalments will take the pressure off for the time being. When the debtor pays the first instalment you should thank them profusely and then make a courteous telephone call before the next instalment is due. Once the debtor gets into the habit of paying the instalments your chances of full recovery are excellent. I would always recommend such an arrangement in preference to legal proceedings as the law is costly and involves long delays. Even at the end of a drawn-out court case, the result will often be an arrangement for the debtor to pay by instalments. If you make an arrangement with the debtor for payment by instalments, you should immediately confirm the arrangement in writing. Letter 9.7 is a simple but sensible communication to the debtor.

9.7   Letter confirming payment by instalments

Mr O. D. Account
452 Credit Place
DEBTORS VALLEY STA 26477

Dear Mr Account,

We refer to recent discussions regarding our outstanding account of $1200 and note the arrangement for you to pay the amount due by an initial instalment of $200 followed by monthly instalments of $100 payable on the last day of each month.

We confirm that this arrangement is satisfactory and we look forward to receiving your cheque for the initial instalment of $200 by return mail.

Yours sincerely,
Business Afloat Corporation

A M Buoyant

A. M. Buoyant (Ms)
Accounts Manager

Collecting unpaid debts

In the absence of an arrangement with your debtor to pay by instalments, you must decide what to do about an unpaid account. The first option is to write the debt off, which you may be inclined to do if the amount is comparatively small. If you are in the happy position of deriving a tax advantage from the write-off, so much the better. The second option is to place the debt in the hands of a collection agency. Collection agencies will usually negotiate with you to share the spoils of the amount recovered. The third option is to seek legal advice. Solicitors charge on a fee-for-time basis and you should therefore satisfy yourself you have a good claim and that the debtor is reasonably financial should you secure judgment. If you lose you will probably be ordered to pay the debtor's costs. More will be said in the next chapter about court actions.

Many people in business believe no stone should be left unturned in the search for innovative ways to recover unpaid debts. They spend their waking hours searching the precedents and trying to understand how common thieves are allowed to escape gaol for failing to pay their bills. Once I knew a dentist who dealt with the problem of unpaid bills by allowing his patients the benefit of credit, but strictly on conditions set out in a letter accompanying his accounts. The dentist wrote Letter 9.8 to his patients.

9.8   Credit surcharge letter

Mr I. Tooth
27 Molar Place
DENTURETOWN STA 26322

Dear Mr Tooth,

I am enclosing my account for dental treatment carried out at my surgery and you will see that the amount due is $120. This amount includes a surcharge of $20 for credit.

If you would prefer not to take advantage of my credit facility, I will be pleased to accept payment of $100 within fourteen (14) days in full settlement of the account. Payment after fourteen (14) days should include the credit surcharge of $20.

Yours sincerely,

(signature)

I. Pullam (Dr)

Technically, the dentist is not entitled to add $20 to his account for the privilege of credit. Nevertheless, a very high proportion of his accounts were paid within fourteen days, and presumably his patients found it easier to pay quickly than argue about the surcharge. The lesson in the letter from the dentist is you are entitled to offer a discount for early settlement of an account, but it must be a genuine discount and not the result of inflating the cost of the service.

If you are owed money by a company rather than an individual, this is good and bad news. The bad news is the company may be worth nothing and you are left whistling in the wind for your money. Most companies have limited liability and shareholders

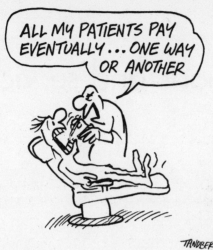

are not responsible for the debts of the company. Directors may be liable where debts are incurred at a time when a reasonable person would know that the company cannot meet its liabilities, but this is difficult to prove. The good news is a simple procedure exists under section 459E of the Corporations Law to put pressure on a company that refuses to pays its debts.

Provided the debt exceeds $2000 you can serve a statutory demand on the company in the prescribed form, and if the company does not pay the debt within 21 days, it will be deemed to be insolvent. A debtor company can apply to a court to set aside your statutory demand if it can demonstrate that a genuine dispute exists over the debt. If the company is sailing close to the wind, however, it will want to appease you and deal with your demand within 21 days, otherwise you can apply to the court for an order winding up the company. Unfortunately, this procedure for dealing with a company debt is not available if court proceedings have already been commenced. The next chapter includes a section on court actions about defective goods and unsatisfactory services.

Chapter Ten

Goods and services

Protecting consumers

You are probably aware that three elements are required for an enforceable contract: offer, acceptance and consideration. It is also a requirement that a level playing field exists between the parties to a contract. In other words, the common law assumes each party enters the contract freely and will benefit equally from the arrangement. But the common law was developed before the advent of large corporations, many of them operating on a global basis. Consumers of goods and services provided by large corporations do not have equal understanding of the issues involved in a dispute, or access to the marble and glass offices of fancy law firms to advise them. For this reason State, Commonwealth and Territory governments operate Consumer Affairs Departments to protect consumers and provide a forum to enable them to exercise their rights and enforce their remedies against individuals and corporations who provide defective goods and unsatisfactory services.

Consumer protection laws and consumer claims tribunals now safeguard the rights of citizens, filling the vacuum left by judges of the common law, who once championed the rights of individuals by protecting them against the monarch and the noble classes. Judges today show little concern for citizens' rights, focusing their minds on precedent and the rule of law in a way that often reflects the values of the corporate giants. Just as the major political parties now run the agendas of the large corporations, so too the courts—the judicial arm of government—frequently promote corporate values in a way that our forebears could never have imagined. In the United States and Canada, for example, the Bill of Rights and Charter of Rights and Freedoms respectively have been hijacked by the corporate world to successfully argue that corporate interests represent a higher value than the rights of the individual.

Commonwealth, and State and Territory consumer protection laws are designed to enhance common law rights, and so the common law defences for breach of contract are generally available under the relevant legislation. These defences include mistake, misrepresentation, duress and undue influence. More specifically, the Commonwealth Trade Practices Act (TPA) protects consumers against misleading and deceptive conduct, unconscionable conduct and unjust contracts. It also implies certain conditions and warranties into consumer contracts, including a requirement that goods and services must not be substandard. Similar consumer protection laws have been passed by State and Territory parliaments including the Fair Trading Act.

Sometimes a State or Territory government will introduce a law reducing or extinguishing the rights of consumers to enforce legal remedies (usually to assist large corporations) and then the consumer would need to rely on Commonwealth consumer protection laws. The State government, for example, might pass a law affecting your right to claim compensation for a defective mortgage product designed and marketed by the government. In such a case you would need to rely on the TPA to assert your right to protection against misleading and deceptive conduct or the implied condition of a consumer contract that goods must be reasonably fit for their intended purpose. Under the Australian Constitution, any conflict between State and Commonwealth law is resolved in favour of the Commonwealth law, and so federal judges could use the TPA to defeat the attempt by the State government to limit your right to compensation for the defective mortgage product.

If you were to take on a State or Territory government under the Commonwealth trade practices legislation, you would need to make your case in the Federal Court. You might know other consumers who have similar problems with the State government's mortgage product. Theoretically you can join together with these other consumers in a class action against the government. One problem you would encounter is an increasing reluctance by State and federal judges to allow consumers to bring class actions, which were intended as a cost effective means for large numbers of people with similar claims to gain access to the justice system. Judges now define a 'class' so narrowly that the biblical image of a camel and the eye of a needle comes readily to mind.

Another problem for the prospective class action is the legal aid system, set up and run by the same State government you are hoping to sue for the defective mortgage product. As a matter of public policy you should be entitled to legal aid if you have a good cause of action and meet the eligibility criteria. You can expect a government to be reluctant to fund an action against itself, however. An important feature of legal aid in New South Wales is your entitlement to a costs indemnity if you lose the case. Should you run your case against the government without a costs indemnity and lose, you would normally be ordered to pay the government's legal bill. This principle of a costs indemnity where you have a good cause of action ought to apply in other areas of the law besides legal aid cases, but that is a subject worthy of a separate book.

Defective goods

My brother-in-law proudly manufactures electrical components in Australia and frequently quotes former American President Harry Truman in the context of quality control: 'The buck stops here.' If you were to buy an electrical component from my brother-in-law, you can be sure it was tested, re-examined and double-checked before it left the factory. Most small businesses pride themselves on the standard of their work, and if you had a serious problem with a local manufacturer, it would be an unusual circumstance in my experience. Where a problem does arise, the first step in seeking a refund of your money or compensation for defective goods is to contact the retailer or supplier (whoever sold you the goods) and point out the defect. Consumer laws require the goods to meet the following standards:

1. *They should fit their description*. This means the supplier's description and your description in the order to the supplier.

2. *They should be suitable for their intended purpose.* The purpose must be communicated to the supplier when placing the order, unless the purpose is obvious from the nature of the goods, in which case the intended purpose is implied in the order.

3. *They should be of merchantable quality.* This is the general responsibility on manufacturers and suppliers of goods to provide goods that are similar in quality and similar in function to other goods of the same type. For instance, a submerged water pump that rusted would not be of merchantable quality; a new motor vehicle that continually broke down would not be of merchantable quality.

4. *They should correspond with a sample.* If you buy from a sample, the goods you receive should look the same as the sample and be of similar quality to the sample.

The supplier of defective goods may not be prepared to consider a refund of your money or compensation, but may instead offer you replacement goods. Provided those goods are similar to the goods in your original order, you would be obliged to accept them. Also bear in mind you are not entitled to a refund, replacement goods or compensation if the supplier told you about the faults when you purchased the goods. For instance, defective goods are often sold as 'seconds', and no question would arise of receiving a refund or compensation for goods already discounted on account of their defective or damaged condition. Perhaps you would get replacement goods for a serious defect, but this would depend more on your powers of persuasion than your legal rights. A deposit is generally part of the purchase price for goods and would not normally be refundable. Even a 'holding' deposit is not refundable in the absence of a written agreement to the contrary.

You need to distinguish between breach of a condition of a consumer contract and breach of a warranty. A condition is a fundamental term of the contract and breach of a condition entitles you to return the defective goods. Breach of a warranty is less destructive of the contract and you must retain the defective goods and claim compensation. New products will sometimes include a guarantee or warranty card that requires a consumer to register their name and address to receive additional rights over and above rights guaranteed under consumer laws. Most commonly these guarantees or warranties offer replacement goods where no legal obligation exists to do so. Extended warranty protection is frequently offered in the motor vehicle industry on top of the dealer's statutory warranty obligations. If you buy a vehicle from a motor dealer you receive a statutory warranty that defects appearing within a certain time will be repaired. The warranty does not apply in the case of a vehicle more than ten years old or one that has travelled more than 160 000 kilometres, and no warranties are applicable to a vehicle sold privately.

When you write to the supplier of defective goods, remember that the person responsible is unlikely to have deliberately set out to mislead you. No manufacturer, large or small, can afford to market defective goods, and both the supplier and the manufacturer will want to fix the problem as quickly as possible and get on with their businesses. On this basis you should avoid anger and aggression in your letter. State the problem in precise terms and by all means nominate a solution. Personally, I am not averse to indignation in a letter to a person who sells defective goods, but you need to use moderate language. If you purchased through an agent, send a copy of your letter to the agent. Some doubt may exist as to whether the supplier, manufacturer, wholesaler or retailer is responsible for the defect. In such a case you would send copies of your letter down the line, but be careful not to defame anyone. Letter 10.1 is a general letter to a supplier of defective goods.

10.1 Letter to manufacturer

Ms A. Widget
General Manager
Widget Manufacturing Company
234 Industrial Park Drive
SILVER CITY STA 27666

Dear Ms Widget,

I am obliged to place in writing those concerns I outlined to you on the telephone a few days ago. I had hoped in the interim you might have done something about the defective widgets you supplied, but no such luck. My concerns are as follows:

* the widgets were designed for square holes and my widget holes are circular;
* circular widgets should include round caps;
* you supplied plastic widgets when I specified high tensile steel; and
* the order form refers to 50 units not 50 boxes.

Needless to say, I am extremely concerned that such a small job includes so many faults, raising serious questions about your manufacturing standards. Apart from the quality of the work, the job has taken you twice as long as expected, and to add insult to injury, you are quite nonchalant when I question you about the delay.

I am at a loss to know why you bothered to supply such grossly defective goods. In any event, unless you provide widgets according to my company's specification without delay, I intend engaging another manufacturer and charging the cost to your account.

Yours faithfully,
Pee Veed Seed Company

I. M. Peeved

I. M. Peeved (Mr)
New Products Manager

There are a number of options available if you cannot resolve a dispute with a supplier or manufacturer of defective goods.

Private consumer organisations and your local Consumer Affairs Department will carry out investigations. If these inquiries are unsuccessful, you can make a formal complaint to the relevant consumer tribunal, or commence court proceedings for loss and damage. In the commercial world where you have an on-going trade with suppliers or manufacturers, you will generally want to settle disputes privately rather than disrupt your trade arrangements.

My brother-in-law says you should always maintain control of a situation so that at the height of a dispute, when critical decisions need to be made, you are holding either the goods or the money, and preferably both. He says he never allows himself to get into a situation where he must sue to recover the cost of defective goods. Apart from scrupulously checking the manufactured goods that leave his factory, my brother-in-law gives the same close attention to anything that arrives at his loading dock before he parts with his money. He suggested Letter 10.2 in response to the above letter.

10.2 Reply from manufacturer

Mr I. M. Peeved
New Products Manager
Pee Veed Seed Company
122 Hollyoak Avenue
SILVER CITY STA 27666

Dear Mr Peeved,

Thank you for your recent letter expressing concern about my widgets.

I do regret the delay filling your order, but widgets seem to be in great demand at the moment. You will also appreciate that supplying you with 50 boxes instead of 50 units (an error for which I accept full responsibility) has seriously disrupted my production program. With your permission I will send a truck tomorrow for the excess stock.

You may not be aware circular widget holes are outdated. In fact, they have not been used in the industry this century to the best of my knowledge. I am taking the liberty of enclosing the latest square widget holes with my compliments, and I think you will find they make a remarkable difference to the efficiency and performance of the widgets.

As with the circular widgets, round caps are rarely used these days, and one of the benefits of the new square caps is they help secure the widget holes to the wall of the holding tank. This in turn gives purchase to the line pump and cuts running costs by more than half. I am sure you will be delighted with the square caps.

As for the 'plastic' widgets, in fact, they are lightweight colour bonded titanium, and represent state of the art refined metal technology. They are stronger than high tensile steel and have twice the life span. You will also be pleased to know that both metals are in good supply and their refinement costs are comparable.

Please return the new widgets if they are not to your complete satisfaction and I will arrange a credit note at the earliest opportunity.

Yours sincerely,
Widget Manufacturing Company

A. widget

A. Widget (Ms)
General Manager

One useful State and Territory consumer law is the Contracts Review Act which boosts the consumer protection given under the Commonwealth trade practices legislation by enabling a court to free a consumer who is locked into an unjust contractual obligation. For example, the Contracts Review Act may defeat a written agreement which includes a clause excluding a person from liability for negligence if it can be shown that a supplier failed to draw a consumer's attention to the exclusion clause. Perhaps the most significant feature of all consumer protection laws is that no requirement exists to prove that a supplier of goods or services acted fraudulently or negligently. It is sufficient to show that you suffered loss or damage as a result of relying on the conduct complained of in order to recover compensation for your loss or damage.

Unsatisfactory services

Like manufacturers of goods, people in service industries have a similar responsibility to consumers in that the services must be performed properly. Consumer laws require service providers to meet the following standards:

1. *To act professionally*. If you engage somebody to perform a service in return for a fee, that person must be competent to perform the service.
2. *To charge a reasonable fee*. In the absence of a fee fixed by the controlling body of the profession or industry, the fee charged must be reasonable, having regard to similar charges for similar services.
3. *To act expeditiously*. An inordinate delay in performing the service will render any contract with the consumer unenforceable.
4. *To be responsible for employees*. Employers will be held responsible for unprofessional or negligent acts of employees.

Contracts for services also include certain warranties under the trade practices legislation that cannot be excluded by the service provider. These warranties are that services must be provided with due care and skill; materials used in connection with the service must be reasonably fit for the purpose; and the service must be appropriate where the consumer has made known the purpose or results to be achieved. Because they are warranties and not conditions, you are entitled only to damages for breach of contract, and no right exists to terminate the contract. The warranties do not apply to insurance contracts, and industry and professional bodies usually have supplementary rules or codes of conduct that vary the warranties, often imposing strict obligations on members to deal fairly with consumers.

Sometimes unscrupulous repairers will use second-hand materials and you will wonder why the repair job is short-lived. One of the benefits of greater consumer awareness is that repairers are more conscious of the standard of their work than they were a few years ago. Consumer organisations have access to specialist scientific equipment to evaluate machinery parts, and many private engineering companies will prepare reports as to whether or not parts are second-hand. Assuming you have suitable evidence, you are entitled to compensation from a company or individual using second-hand parts in a repair job when you have been charged for new parts, or might reasonably have expected to get new parts. You should write to the repairer and indicate the problem with the goods repaired. You will immediately be aware of your difficulties if you have no binding agreement with the repairer and Letter 10.3 assumes an earlier letter confirming a contract (see Letter 5.3 on page 105).

10.3 Letter to repairer

Mr S. O. Cold
General Manager
Ice Cold Refrigeration Company
34 Frozen Way
CHILLY HILL STA 22440

Dear Mr Cold,

On 31 January this year you completed repair work on my refrigerator and you were duly paid for the work. You guaranteed parts and workmanship for a period of three (3) months as noted in my letter dated 10 January.

Although a period in excess of three months has elapsed since the work was completed, I wish to inform you that the refrigerator has again broken down, and following an examination of the parts you replaced by Whitegoods Refrigeration Limited, it is revealed that the repairs were not carried out properly.

In particular, you replaced the thermostat with a second-hand thermostat which has collapsed, therefore causing the present breakdown. I am enclosing a copy of a report from Whitegoods Refrigeration Limited together with a copy of an account from the company.

In the circumstances I require a full refund of the sum of $250 paid to you, plus compensation of $150, being the amount charged by Whitegoods Refrigeration Limited to replace the second-hand thermostat with a new thermostat. The total amount due is $400 and I require your cheque within fourteen (14) days.

Yours faithfully,

Y. Repair

Y. Repair (Ms)

The author of this letter has the basis for a claim. Without the original letter to the repairer, however, you cannot prove the terms of the contract, and I emphasise that you should get something in writing when you are dealing with service industries. After the event you will be astounded how everybody seems to suffer from memory loss, and it will often be a case of your word against the repairer, which is not a case at all. Oral contracts are binding, but the onus is on you to prove the contract, and you will probably need something in writing to corroborate your claim.

In the present case the main difficulty is that the repairer has not specifically agreed to use new parts in the repair job. The original letter did not specify whether new or second-hand parts were to be used, and the repairer might argue that in normal circumstances (in repair jobs of a similar type), second-hand parts are usually used and are generally adequate. A repairer must act professionally and charge a reasonable fee. If they can do so using second-hand parts, no requirement exists to use new parts, provided the job is adequate. You might expect to receive Letter 10.4 from the repairer.

10.4   Reply from repairer

Ms Y. Repair
624 Maintenance Drive
CHILLY HILL STA 22440

Dear Ms Repair,

We refer to your letter claiming compensation and a refund of moneys paid for repairs to your Model T. Refrigerator and reply as follows:

- Your refrigerator was in bad repair and we suggested, in view of its age, that it be replaced with a new model.
- Despite our advice, you indicated we should do the best we could for the amount of money you were prepared to spend, namely $250, and repair the refrigerator.
- We undertook to 'repair or replace' the thermostat, but at no stage did we promise a new thermostat.

The replacement thermostat was second-hand, as indicated in the report accompanying your letter, but in our experience second-hand thermostats are generally adequate, and it is normal practice in the refrigerator repair industry to use second-hand materials, particularly where refrigerators are old and customers are anxious to keep the cost of repairs to a minimum.

As stated in your letter dated 10 January, the refrigerator operated satisfactorily for a period of three months, and this period represents the extent of our guarantee. In the circumstances we have no alternative but to reject your claim, and any proceedings will be strongly defended.

Yours faithfully,
Ice Cold Refrigeration Company

S. O. Cold

S. O. Cold (Mr)
General Manager

A more amenable repairer might suggest a compromise, perhaps offering to pay for the cost of replacing the thermostat. Others might simply ignore you and this may provoke you to take further action. Most repairers need to be licensed and you can write to the appropriate licensing authority or the controlling body of the relevant industry. You can also contact your local consumer affairs department. If you have a genuine complaint about a person in any service industry and you are diligent enough to record the transaction in writing, there is no end to the aggravation you can cause.

The ultimate remedy against anybody providing unsatisfactory services is to withhold payment, as services are rarely paid for in advance. You can demand that the service be performed properly, and failing that, you can engage somebody else to do the job. You must give the original service provider the opportunity to perform the service properly, however, otherwise you will still be responsible for their account.

Court action

The biblical imperative to settle your disputes before going to court remains true today, even when you sincerely believe you are right. You can never be sure in a drawn-out court case what issues might arise to defeat your claim. Some insignificant fact or obscure precedent may be presented to the court and suddenly the judge sees your claim in a completely different light. In the civil jurisdiction, judges make their decisions on the balance of probabilities and, most significantly, costs generally follow the verdict. Not only might you lose the case, but you will also face a legal bill presented by your opponent that is likely to choke a horse.

When people ask me how would I reform the legal system, I always give the same answer: put all the law on computer. We could revolutionise the legal system by keying into a computer every case and every statute applicable to a particular jurisdiction, and then ask the computer to make a preliminary decision based on the facts of your case. With the benefit of the computer's preliminary decision, you could then approach a court for a final decision, but without the penalty of an adverse costs order if you lose. This is the costs indemnity principle I referred to earlier. In other words, your certificate from the computer would state that on the balance of probabilities you are likely to win the case, and therefore you should not pay the added penalty of the other party's costs if subsequently you lose. Law reform on this scale would provide access to justice for ordinary people almost overnight.

If you are obliged to commence court action, most claims for recovery of business debts fall within one or more of the following categories: goods sold and delivered; moneys due and owing; work done and materials supplied; and services rendered. In New South Wales you can now bring an action in the Small Claims Division of the Local Court for up to $10 000 without the risk of losing an arm and a leg in legal fees. Previously, the limit was $3000. This jurisdiction is designed as a cheap and simple method of recovering debts with a minimum of fuss and, most significantly, without the intervention of lawyers.

Once your summons is filed in court you must serve a copy on the defendant. Where the defendant is an individual, the summons must be served personally. Make sure you do not serve the summons yourself as this could be prohibited under local law. In any event you will want to avoid direct contact with the defendant in case you aggravate the situation. Obtain the services of a mercantile agent or arrange for the court sheriff to serve the summons. If the defendant is a company you can serve the summons by registered mail addressed to the registered office of the company.

If you are the defendant and you have a defence to the claim by the plaintiff (or even if you have no defence), you are entitled to further and better particulars of the claim. The form of the request for further and better particulars demonstrates the potential complexity of court proceedings and the need to keep lawyers out of straightforward consumer disputes if a level playing field is to be maintained. Most of the information in the request for further and better particulars is excessive, but you are entitled to full details of the plaintiff's claim. You will certainly put a cat among the plaintiff's pigeons with Letter 10.5 or any similar request.

No guarantee exists that your request for further and better particulars will prevent the plaintiff from signing judgment.

10.5   Request for further particulars

Ms A. Widget
General Manager
Widget Manufacturing Company
234 Industrial Park Drive
SILVER CITY STA 27666

Dear Ms Widget,

I refer to the summons received by registered post for goods sold and delivered, and I would be grateful if you could supply me with the following further and better particulars of your claim:

1.   Do the goods sold and delivered relate to an agreement between us, express or implied?

2. If express or partly express:
    (a) was the agreement made orally or in writing; or
    (b) partly oral and partly in writing?
3. If oral:
    (a) specify, giving date, time and place, when and where the agreement was made;
    (b) identify, giving names and addresses, the person or persons on behalf of your company and our company respectively to whom and by whom the agreement was made; and
    (c) what was said?
4. If in writing:
    (a) to whom was the writing directed and by whom; and
    (b) where may the document or documents be inspected?
5. If the agreement was partly oral and partly in writing, furnish the particulars requested in paragraphs three and four above in respect of the written and oral portions respectively.
6. If implied:
    (a) what are the facts and circumstances alleged that give rise to such implication?
    (b) what are the alleged implied terms?
    (c) do you rely upon any statutes or regulations which it is alleged imply terms into the alleged agreement?
    (d) if so, identify all such statutes and regulations; and
    (e) specify such implied terms.
7. If more than one agreement is alleged, furnish particulars requested in the above paragraphs in respect of each agreement.

Pending my receipt of the above further and better particulars, I take it you will extend to me the usual courtesy, and time in which a defence must be filed will not run. Should this not be the position please inform me by return and I will notify the court of this request.

Yours faithfully,
Pee Veed Seed Company

I. M. Peeved

I. M. Peeved (Mr)
New Products Manager

You should file your defence within the time prescribed by the summons. If you are not in a position to file your defence, the least you should do is notify the court. A telephone call is not usually sufficient. Send a short note or letter, advising that you have requested further and better particulars, or call at the court and advise of your request personally. The court has no obligation to notify you if the plaintiff attempts to sign judgment. You may be lucky enough to strike a compassionate court officer who sends the plaintiff away until the request for further and better particulars is answered. The benefit of your request for further and better particulars lies in your application to set judgment aside. The court will take a dim view of the plaintiff's enthusiasm for judgment while the request for further and better particulars is outstanding, and you will normally get an order setting judgment aside, provided you have a prima facie defence to the claim.

The best way to handle a defence is to consult a lawyer and incorporate everything he or she tells you in the appropriate notice of defence, but only after converting it to simple English. Even in an age of rampant bush lawyers, drafting your own defence to a summons is perilous. It is also quite unnecessary for two reasons. First, there are numerous free legal services available to assist you. Second, most lawyers will be happy to advise you and charge at their normal hourly rate rather than run the case in a court where they are not recognised and cannot recover their fees. If you decide to handle the case yourself without consulting a lawyer, say nothing more in your defence than 'the defendant is not indebted to the plaintiff as alleged' and throw yourself on the mercy of the court. As I said earlier, your defence must incorporate everything you intend raising at the hearing, and if you do not know all the issues, it is best to say as little as possible.

Before the hearing the plaintiff or the defendant is free to make an offer of settlement. Ninety per cent of cases are settled before the hearing, and some even settle during the hearing. The offer of settlement may be oral, but it is better to communicate the offer in writing. Be sure to head your letter 'Without Prejudice' otherwise it might be construed as an admission of liability. Chapter Two includes further information about 'Without Prejudice' letters.

Chapter Eleven

Advertising

Advertising in the mass media

Many of us avoid products and services simply because they are advertised on radio and television or fill the pages of newspapers. We are appalled that advertisers would intrude into our private lives with their attention-seeking commercials as if we were representative of the markets to which their campaigns are directed. The fact is, however, we are fair game in the world of advertising, and market research confirms that advertising is effective and increases sales. Advertisers have a difficult job in that campaigns directed towards those of us who resent commercials would not sell products or services. Perhaps tighter controls ought to be placed on the industry and the standard of commercials raised, but the advertisers argue, and reasonably, that their job is to sell products and services, not to educate people.

Once we come to terms with the reality of advertising in a free market, the judicious use of radio and television commercials can create opportunities and provide unexpected rewards for those of us marketing goods and services. We can also play our own small part in raising the standard of advertising by adopting ethical practices in our campaigns.

The courts have long recognised that advertisers exaggerate certain features of their products and services in order to achieve sales. 'Let the buyer beware' is a legal principle often forgotten in the rush towards greater consumer protection laws. This principle still guides the courts and the terms of a statute need to accurately state the obligations imposed on an advertiser if judges are to assist consumers of goods and services. By and large the courts will rely on the buyer beware principle to reinforce the common law.

One reason for the proliferation of consumer tribunals and alternative dispute resolution services is a reluctance by the courts to move away from the adversarial notion that each party to a dispute is entitled to bring to the contest whatever resources it has available. Clearly the ordinary consumer is no match for global corporations. Large companies influence governments in a way that citizens can match only for a fleeting moment at the ballot box. And invariably the alternative government will be subjected to more of the same corporate influence, given that large corporations contribute more or less equally to the coffers of the major political parties.

Misleading and deceptive advertising

Section 52 of the Trade Practices Act (TPA) relies on the dictionary definitions of 'misleading' and 'deceptive' to require all advertising in trade or commerce to comply with certain standards. Private advertisements by individuals selling products or services will not normally be affected unless you are carrying on a business. Also, political and religious advertisements are not regarded as publications in trade or commerce. Community and environmental activities may be caught by the legislation where the advertisements will benefit a commercial operator involved in business. As with loss and damage for defective goods and unsatisfactory services, an intention to mislead or deceive is not necessary to breach the statutory provision as it applies to advertising.

Some expressions such as 'the best in the world' or 'the smartest in town' are not misleading in the sense that customers are not misled because such claims are obvious exaggerations and are recognised for what they are. We often see the claim 'the best that money can buy', and if you were able to buy something better you would have no redress against the company or individual making the claim. On the other hand, a claim that certain lawnmowers were 'the best new mowers in town' would be patently false if the mowers were actually reconditioned models. The advertiser would be in breach of Section 52 of the TPA and could be ordered to pay compensation for loss or damage.

Your claim that a particular product or service is 'on special' at 25 per cent below the recommended retail price will be misleading if the going rate in the industry is 25 per cent below the recommended retail price. More obvious is a claim that your product or service is selling 'below cost' if it is not true. Free gifts and prizes are also common bedmates with misleading advertising. Legislation in some States and Territories prohibits such offers. It is misleading to offer gifts or prizes and at the same time inflate the price of goods or services to cover the cost of the gifts or prizes.

Other troubles to avoid in undertaking your own advertising campaign concern 'bait advertising'. You are not entitled to attract customers with a 'bait' advertisement and then 'switch' the buyer to something else. For instance, you cannot advertise a 'special end-of-season sale' and then inform prospective customers that the season is over but they might like to look at your new range. Another dangerous gimmick is to advertise a product or service, and once you have the customers in the door, inform them you are out of stock and try to interest them in something else. As you might know, an advertisement is a mere 'invitation to treat' and not a contract. But if the advertisement is false, misleading or deceptive, your publication may be an invitation to the Australian Competition and Consumer Commission (ACCC) to knock on your door.

At this stage you may be having second thoughts about the earth-shattering campaign you had prepared for your new product or service. Your well-deserved satisfaction at seeing your product in the market will be short-lived if your first customer is an officer of the ACCC. My advice if you have no experience in marketing is to consult the professionals, particularly if your product or service needs a bit of jazzing up (no offence intended). We are living in an age of specialisation and most products and services require specialist marketing skills to achieve maximum impact with your advertising campaign.

Sometimes you may be unable to supply customers for reasons beyond your control. Excessive demand may mean you are out of stock and if so, you should make satisfactory arrangements with your customers because you may be in breach of the advertising laws if you cannot supply advertised goods or services. A number of options exist under the TPA including making arrangements to supply the customer within a reasonable time; offering to supply an equivalent product at the same price; and organising for another company to supply the same product at the same price or a similar product at a reasonable price. Of course, you must do as the customer wishes to comply with the TPA, and if the customer rejects all the above options, you still have a problem. If you have taken an order and/or deposit, you should write to your customer and explain the position. Use Letter 11.1 as a guide.

11.1   Letter to customer

Ms V. G. Customer
24 Safe Way
TRADETOWN STA 21622

Dear Ms Customer,

Recently you placed an order with our company for the supply of our Top Dog Executive Office Suite which we listed for sale at $2400 for all orders placed in the month of June. Unfortunately, demand for the suite far exceeded our expectations, and we are unable to supply you at present.

The Top Dog Suite is manufactured in Sweden and we expected our existing stock would be adequate to meet the demand following our June sale. Needless to say, the sale was more successful than expected. Our salesman who took your order was unaware the order could not be filled, and we apologise for this error for which our management is wholly responsible.

Inquiries of the manufacturer in Sweden indicate that the Top Dog range is under review. Two other distributors operate in Australia and we are checking whether they have stock. Failing that, Sverige Australia has a similar range of Executive Office Suites, which you may care to view, and I understand the price is competitive.

We sincerely regret our inability to fill your order at this time, and perhaps you would be willing to call our office to discuss your requirements. Your deposit is fully refundable.

Yours sincerely,
Swedenfurn Design Company

Bjorn Credenza
General Manager

The author of this letter has several problems. He must avoid any suggestion that he deliberately misled the customer, and to do this he must not attempt to switch the customer to another product, if that product is not equivalent to the advertised product. Price may be the only barrier to supplying the product at a later date, and then he would be obliged to carry any loss himself.

If he could get a similar product elsewhere, perhaps from a competitor, he can do that, or at least refer the customer to the competitor. Most important of all, he should leave his options open, which he does in the last paragraph of the letter, as refunding the customer's deposit will not itself absolve him from responsibility for the misleading advertisement.

Advertising Standards Bureau

Complaints about advertising should be directed to the Advertising Standards Bureau (formerly the Advertising Standards Council) in your capital city. Telephone the bureau before launching your missive as a system of self-regulation for the advertising industry in Australia has created a plethora of organisations responsible for the media, which means you may need to complain to more than one body. Self-regulation in advertising is not unlike self-regulation in the legal profession in that the complaints process is inherently biased against consumers. Any organisation that is judge and jury of its own members will always approach questions of conduct and discipline of the members with an eye on self-preservation of the organisation. For years I have complained about shonky lawyers and appalling media advertising, and the score so far is self-regulatory bodies 100 not out, while I am yet to score a run.

My latest foray into the world of advertising concerned an erotic billboard on a city freeway that was a nightmare for motorists. For about 100 metres on either side of the billboard, not one male driver was watching the road. I wrote and complained to the advertising regulator and my complaint was duly considered and dismissed. Not satisfied, I wrote again to the regulator seeking reasons for the decision, and a modified version of my letter is now part of the WriteQuick letter writing program. If you key in 'Advertising Agency' and 'Letter to Regulator', Letter 11.2 will appear on your computer screen.

11.2 Letter to regulator

Ms C. U. Moore
Investigations Manager
Advertising Standards Bureau
66 Benchmark Boulevard
CAPITAL CITY STA 26200

Dear Ms Moore,

Inquiries of your office indicate that on May 10 last you considered a number of complaints (including my own) about a certain billboard on City Road. It was generally alleged that the billboard exploits young women's sexuality in order to sell hair-care products. Questions of road safety were also raised.

You determined that the advertisement was not offensive and demeaning to women, neither portraying them as sex objects nor degrading them. Further, you came to the conclusion that the advertisement was 'sexy' but not 'sexist'. You would not consider the road safety question as it is outside your area of responsibility.

Responding to some of the complaints, the advertiser has said that the advertisement was created by a female design team with the intention of selling the products to women. If that is so, the appropriate place for the advertisement is women's magazines, not boldly displayed on a public thoroughfare, exaggerating its impact and offensiveness.

For me, the billboard advertisement remains offensive and I am not comforted in any way by your ruling. You say it is not your job to determine the appropriateness of the creative concept, but merely to determine whether an advertisement breaches the prevailing community standards. How do you judge those standards?

According to my straw poll of public perceptions, more than half the people I spoke to still find the billboard offensive and I would like to see it removed.

Yours faithfully,

J.R.U. Blue

T. R. U. Blue (Mr)

Direct mail advertising

Direct mail is not to be confused with mail order. If you have something to sell and you write a letter to your prospective customer about your product or service, that is direct mail. Usually your letter will be accompanied by a brochure, and you will invite prospective customers to fill out an order form requesting the product or service, or further information. If the product or service has a low price tag (usually less than $100) you might expect to receive orders on the strength of your letter and brochure. For an expensive product or service, the most you can expect from your direct mail letter is that it will serve as an introduction. You can expect to achieve a sale only when you have secured a personal interview with your prospective customer. Mail order, on the other hand, is not directed at individuals. The product or service is exposed to the public at large through newspaper advertisements or handbills. This book is about writing letters, and so I will deal only with direct mail.

Before you embark on your direct mail campaign, it is imperative to work out a budget and decide how much you are going to spend. Direct mail is very expensive and to begin with you should limit your risk. For instance, the first edition of this book was sold almost entirely by direct mail, and each letter cost about one dollar. I sent 15 000 letters at a total cost of $15 000 made up as follows:

Printing letters	$2000
Printing brochures	$3500
Printing envelopes	$1500
Postage 15 000 @ $0.23 each approx.	$3500
Postage 600 @ $1.15 each approx.	$700
Additional office staff	$2500
Lease of additional word processor	$1300
TOTAL	$15 000

I have not allowed in the figures for fixed overheads such as rent and electricity as I was already committed to those expenses to run my law practice. The item 'Postage 600' represents postage on books sold. Six hundred is the break-even point—600 sales at the unit price of $24.95 is about $15 000. Six hundred sales on a mailing of 15 000 is four per cent return. Sometimes I did better than four per cent, but this is an unusually high return for direct mail, and I was making no profit at four per cent. Your success or failure in direct mail will depend on three variables: the market, the mail list and the mail piece. If all three work, your direct mail advertising campaign will be successful, but if any one of the three is not up to scratch you can expect to lose your money.

The way to improve your direct mail response is to improve one or more of these three variables. You can consult an expert and pay for their advice, or you can use your money to gain your own experience. If you choose the latter course, work on sample mailings, checking all the time on which mailing lists work the best and what copy is the most effective. By way of example, we can look at a mailing for a high-quality bicycle light. Assuming the light sells for $89 and you have a list of 1500 owners of expensive bicycles (you are unlikely to sell an expensive light to the owner of a cheap bike) you must sell eighteen lights to break even because your mailing will cost about $1500. That represents a return of just over one per cent. Your percentage will improve by improving the variables—market, mail list and mail piece. The difficulty with a highly specialised product such as a bicycle light is that the market is fairly restricted. Nevertheless, if your product fulfils a need, you will find a market for it, and Letter 11.3 will test the water.

11.3 Direct mail letter (goods)

Mr B. Pedal
135 Cycle Way
ROAD ISLAND STA 22828

Dear Mr Pedal,

I would like to bring to your attention a new product for bicycles which has revolutionised night riding in Europe. Your safety on the road at night will improve dramatically—visibility will increase by a factor of three. My company has the sole distribution rights in Australia for the NITE LITE, and I guarantee the product will out-perform other bicycle lights available in Australia.

NITE LITE functions either as a front light or rear tail light. Simply change the lens to your requirements. Other advantages of the light include:

(i)   simple attachment to the front or rear of any bicycle;
(ii) compact and secure against theft;
(iii) lightweight aluminium construction; and.
(iv) enhances the performance of your bicycle.

Further information is contained in the attached brochure. You will see that NITE LITE was designed by Heinrich Gurman who designed the ROADSTER FLASH—last year's winner of the Tour de France.

I also draw your attention to the price of NITE LITE. At $89 it represents a modest investment in your safety on the road at night. If you want the best bicycle light in the country, it is a bargain.

If NITE LITE does not out-perform any other bicycle light available in Australia, simply return it within 21 days of delivery, and I will refund your money.

Yours sincerely,
Bicycle Lighting Australia

Rupert J. Speedstar

Rupert J. Speedstar
General Manager

Your accompanying brochure must include a reply coupon. Keep it brief, state the price (do not apologise for the price), offer a free gift or other bonus such as a price reduction or return of goods if not completely satisfied, and offer credit card facilities if possible as this will increase your response rate by up to twenty per cent. Make sure your street address appears somewhere on the order form, otherwise you will look like a fly-by-night. Give your customers the opportunity to order by post, fax, telephone or over the Internet. You will need a secure server for Internet orders and an email contact on your website so that customers can check on the progress of their order and inquire about delivery. The coupon on the following page is simple and effective.

When drafting a direct mail letter, be sure to remember the following:

1. Keep it short—not more than one or two pages—and further information can be detailed in your accompanying brochure.
2. Tell your prospective customer about the benefits of your product or service.
3. Your product or service must be new, revolutionary, cheaper than competitors, better quality, or just plain fantastic.
4. The price must be stated clearly in your letter, brochure and coupon.
5. You should include a bonus with your product or service—for example, free gift, money-back guarantee, or price reduction for immediate reply.
6. Endorsements of your product or service by satisfied customers or public figures will increase your response.

TO: The Marketing Manager
    Bicycle Lighting Australia

Please forward my NITE LITE bicycle light by return post, including interchangeable front and rear lenses. I understand I may return the light within 21 days of delivery if I am not completely satisfied. My payment includes postage and handling within Australia.

NAME_____

ADDRESS _____

_____

☐ Cheque/money order for $89 is enclosed

☐ Debit my

    ☐ Mastercard   ☐ Diners Club

    ☐ Visa Card   ☐ American Express

CARD NUMBER _____

SIGNATURE _____ EXPIRY DATE_____

HOW TO ORDER (choose any one of the following)

-    Post to: Bicycle Lighting Australia,
                   PO Box 374,
                   Mail Centre Capital City STA 26200
-    Fax: (02) 8949 7111
-    Phone: 1800 240 111
-    Internet: www.nitelite.com.au

Bicycle Lighting Australia is a division of Speedstar Cycle Company, 222 Collins Street, Capital City STA 26200.
Member of the Australian Direct Marketing Association.

7. Address your letter personally and do not send circular letters. All your letters may be the same, but each letter should be addressed personally to your prospective customer at their business address.

When you are selling a product or service by direct mail, and the price tag exceeds $100, generally you will need to follow up your direct mail with a personal interview if you expect to make any sales. The direct mail letter serves to introduce you and your product or service, but the real selling will only be done personally. Do not confuse direct mail advertising with selling on the Internet where prospective buyers have the opportunity to scrutinise your product or service and interact with your webpage. A good direct mail campaign supported by the Internet is likely to make an impact.

Sometimes it is not necessary to forward a brochure with your direct mail letter. This is particularly the case if you have an established reputation in a service industry, or your product is already known to prospective customers. You may have a specialised product with a narrow market—if this is the case, you might want to dispense with the brochure. A letter on its own will need added punch, emphasising some feature of your product or service that is the greatest thing since sliced bread. Also, your letter will benefit from examples of the past success of your product or service, and it should conclude with the offer of a free trial or demonstration. Letter 11.4 is a direct mail letter from a company offering a debt-collecting service.

11.4 Direct mail letter (services)

Ms M. Marion
General Manager
Corner Trading Company
55 Barter Place
TRADETOWN STA 21622

Dear Ms Marion,

Many people in business today spend hundreds of hours each year pursuing unpaid debts with limited success. Our company offers a complete debt recovery service and we guarantee the results—we charge a fee only when the debt is recovered.

We have been in the debt recovery business for twenty years and we are experts in our field. By leaving debt recovery to us, you can spend more time in other areas of your business.

Several companies in your industry rely on our debt recovery services, and we have their permission to quote the results of our services:

CLIENT	FULL RECOVERY	PART RECOVERY	NO RECOVERY
Dicey Trading Company	58%	39%	3%
Traders & Merchants Corp.	61%	27%	12%
A. F. & T. S. Trading	65%	25%	10%
Power Exchange Limited	60%	35%	5%
Secure Merchants Corp.	57%	37%	6%

Our representative in your area, John Sheed, will be in touch with you in the next few days, and he will offer you an obligation free demonstration of our debt recovery services.

Yours sincerely,
Professional Debt Recovery Services

Robin Hood

Robin Hood
General Manager

Make sure you have the written permission of your clients to quote statistics and be certain that the clients will recommend your services if approached by your prospective customers. Note the importance of the last paragraph in your letter. The prospective customer has nothing to do. Make an appointment to see them, and arm yourself with a good presentation, preferably a large folder that opens out on a desk, revealing such things as recommendations from existing customers, standard letters of demand, arrangements with solicitors for court proceedings, a list of your charges, and so forth. Experienced firms in the debt recovery business literally sell their presentation—it costs several hundred dollars. If the customer is unable to recover a debt using their methods, these companies then take over the recovery of the debt themselves.

An important aspect of direct mail marketing is the poor old consumer. Some people hate unsolicited mail, particularly what we call 'junk mail'—such things as handbills, unaddressed circular letters and advertising brochures. Recent surveys by market research group Quantum suggest that 75 per cent of people are unhappy with the way businesses collect and sell data, including mailing lists, without our permission. In a belated attempt to catch up with the rest of the world, the Commonwealth government recently introduced National Privacy Principle Guidelines through the office of the federal privacy commissioner. Under the guidelines companies will require your consent before trading private information about you. However, privacy rights, like other citizens' rights, have no real protection in the Australian legal system until we legislate a statutory Bill of Rights in the federal parliament.

Perhaps the last thing that needs to be repeated at the end of this section is that direct mail marketing is very expensive, and at best a long shot if you are doing it yourself. Under no circumstances should you borrow money for direct mail without advice from the marketing experts. You will need to identify your target market and design your mail package, and then you must be able to fill orders. Questions arise about the response rate you can expect and the amount of stock you need on hand. You may

think you have the best product in the world and going into debt is simply one aspect of doing business. Without proper advice, however, you will be left with your loan repayments long after the marketing campaign has run its course.

Chapter Twelve

Real estate

Buying a home

The family home is Australia's sacred cow and we boast the highest proportion of home owners in the world, although the rest of the world is quickly closing the gap. According to *Australian Social Trends 2001*, a report published by the Australian Bureau of Statistics, home ownership has plateaued at 70.1 per cent of households in Australia while in the United Kingdom the figure has risen to 69 per cent and in the United States to 66.8 per cent. In Europe, Germany remains at the bottom of the home ownership list with only 40.5 per cent of households registered on the title to their homes. Home ownership is relatively inexpensive in Australia and the housing industry is an important part of the local economy. Taxation measures that impact on the family home are hugely unpopular in Australia. As a result, the family home is exempt from the GST, land tax, capital gains tax and the list goes on. Any government that makes it difficult to buy and then keep the family home in Australia does so at its peril.

Land title systems vary across Australia, but broadly two types exist. They are loosely described as freehold and strata title.

Freehold title refers to freestanding houses, cottages, terraces and other land holdings where you own the land. Strata title holdings include home units, villas, townhouses and other forms of community title where you own the space and the inside walls of your home, but you share the land with other residents in the development. Another form of unit ownership is company title where you own shares in a company and those shares entitle you to occupy a particular unit. Sometimes people who live in a strata title complex report problems with the body corporate managing the shared or common areas of the development. Retirement villages can also be a nightmare where relations deteriorate between residents and management. In one retirement village complex in Sydney's south west, one-third of the residents were obliged to move out of their homes because of ongoing court battles with the manager of the complex.

When you decide to buy a home, whether it is freehold or strata title, you should employ the services of a lawyer or conveyancer as conveyancing is a high risk business. Claims for professional negligence over conveyancing mistakes have been rising steadily for the past few years and now represent nearly 25 per cent of all notifications to professional indemnity insurers for legal services. Just this week I was asked by the prospective purchaser of a unit in a city apartment block to intervene in a local council decision that would have prevented the purchaser from living in the apartment. The cause of the problem turned out to be the purchaser's lawyer who failed to read a clause in the contract that said the units were zoned as serviced apartments for tourist accommodation and could not be occupied by the owners.

Another reason for the rise in professional negligence claims over conveyancing mistakes is the competitive market in conveyancing. You can pay some lawyers and conveyancers just a few hundred dollars for a transaction that is often extremely complex and time consuming. As a result, some people cut corners on conveyancing because the fee they charge is insufficient to cover their overheads. I suggest you anticipate this problem and secure a contract before you decide on your conveyancing representative. Write to the owner or the owner's agent of the home you want to buy and use Letter 12.1 as a guide.

12.1 Letter requesting contract

Mr A. Vendor
27 Household Drive
HOMETOWN STA 23211

OR

Ms Ann Agent
Principal
Hometown Real Estate
55 Commercial Road
HOMETOWN STA 23211

Dear Mr Vendor [Ms Agent],

I refer to our recent discussions and confirm my offer to purchase your/your client's house at 27 Household Drive, Hometown, for the price of $250 000. The offer is subject to contract and I look forward to receiving the contract at your earliest convenience.

When forwarding the contract, it would assist if you could also forward copies of the following documents which you/your client may have in your/his possession:

(i)   a survey report identifying the buildings on the land in relation to boundaries;
(ii) certificates from the local council as to the zoning of the land and approvals for buildings on the land;
(iii) a certificate from the relevant water and sewerage authorities identifying the location of water mains and sewerage pipes;
(iv) pest inspection reports regarding treatment of the buildings for pests, particularly white ants and borers; and
(v)   a copy of a title search and plan indicating easements or restrictions on the land.

I will let you know the name of my conveyancing representative as soon as possible, but I would be grateful if you could leave the name blank in the contract at this stage. I would be happy to pick up the contract as soon as it is available.

Yours sincerely,

A. Purchase

A. Purchase (Ms)

If you are purchasing a strata or community title property you should also ask the vendor about the body corporate or management company that operates the strata scheme. You will want to know who to contact about the history of the development and any unusual features of the building. The important thing to watch for when buying a unit, strata title or company title property is that the building you are about to inhabit is not on the verge of a large capital expenditure to which you will be required to contribute. This can only be determined by an examination of the books of the body corporate, and you should instruct your lawyer or conveyancer to undertake the appropriate search. Also, there may be special resolutions passed by the body corporate, which limit or negate statutory rules governing the affairs of the building. For instance, you may have strong feelings about animals, and if so, it would be judicious to study the body corporate rules to see if animals are allowed.

Complex questions arise when a strata unit is damaged by water, fire or pest infestation. It seems that you are responsible for the damage if it originated within the walls of your unit. If the problem came through the floor, ceiling or walls from another unit or the common property, the body corporate is responsible. The body corporate is required by legislation to hold an appropriate damages insurance policy with an approved insurer. Buildings must be insured for their replacement or reinstatement value. Individual owners of units need to take out supplementary insurance to cover any shortfall in the body corporate insurance and to avoid arguments about who is responsible for damage in a particular case.

When you receive the contract it will probably include many of the documents in the above letter as vendors are required by law to make full disclosure in a real estate contract. Most people are overwhelmed by the size and complexity of a real estate contract and decide to engage the services of a lawyer or conveyancer from the outset of the conveyancing transaction. If you already have the contract, however, you will have a distinct advantage in terms of negotiating with your lawyer or conveyancer. For example, you might only want something explained that became apparent after reading the contract carefully in your own time—in other words, you don't need the whole document interpreted, given that the full details of the property are to be found in the contract. The lawyer or conveyancer cannot claim additional work as a result of surprises if the contract is available when they give you a quote.

If you do not know a lawyer or conveyancer, the best reference will be a friend or relation who has bought a home and been satisfied with their conveyancing representative. Often, you will be buying through an agent who recommends a particular person for the conveyancing work. An inherent conflict exists in this arrangement, however, because the agent is in fact the vendor's agent. You will be better served if you choose your own conveyancing representative. Once you have decided on your lawyer or conveyancer, and given them the contract to check, I suggest sending them Letter 12.2.

12.2 Instruction to conveyancing representative

Mr N. O. Worries
Licensed Conveyancer
Ace Conveyancing Services
124 Title Boulevard
HOMETOWN STA 23211

Dear Mr Worries,

I refer to our discussion today and note you will undertake the conveyancing work on my purchase at 27 Household Drive, Hometown. You have agreed to do the job for $1650 made up as follows:

Conveyancing fee	$500
General disbursements	$120
Searches and enquiries	$180
Registration fees	$110
Updated survey	$220
Pest inspection report	$170
Building inspection report	$220
Council building certificate	$130
	$1650

Apart from these charges I note your advice that stamp duty of $7240 is the only other expense I will incur. I am not obtaining a mortgage and my money is available at call. It would be convenient if you could give me a few days notice when you require funds.

I confirm that one matter needs your special attention, namely, the proximity of the house to disused cattle sales yards. Would you please make sure no toxic chemical dumps or former cattle dips are located on the land.

Please let me know as soon as your preliminary inquiries are completed as I am anxious to sign the contract as soon as possible.

Yours sincerely,

A Buyer

A. Buyer (Ms)

I would urge you to draw to the attention of your conveyancing representative any unusual feature of the property you are buying and then confirm your instructions in writing. Some of the problems you can have include access to the property, soil contamination, covenants on the land, boundary fences, mine subsidence, council approval to buildings, pest infestation, location of sewerage and water pipes, and the list goes on. Your conveyancing representative will also check the vendor's title and make sure the person selling the property actually owns it. One thing your lawyer or conveyancer will not tell you is what is happening around your property, such as the activities of your prospective neighbours, or the likelihood of your view getting built out. Unless you specifically instruct your conveyancing representative, their inquiries will end at the boundaries of your property.

Again, if you are purchasing a strata or community title property, you will want to alert your conveyancing representative to the need to examine the records of the body corporate. Professional searchers will carry out an inspection of the strata manager's books and give you a report. A good searcher will draw your attention to anything in the minutes of the body corporate meetings that represent an ongoing problem for residents. Apart from unusual expenditure items such as a lift that constantly needs maintenance, the minutes will also reveal other recurring problems such as visitors parking their cars on common areas or disputes between residents about noise.

One aspect of the conveyancing transaction I have not covered is your home mortgage, which is generally an integral part of buying a home. Your conveyancing representative is not qualified to advise you about your mortgage unless they also happen to be an accountant or investment adviser. A prudent lawyer or conveyancer will write to you and make it abundantly clear you need to get other advice about your mortgage. If you do get unsolicited advice from your conveyancing representative about any aspect of your proposed loan, write down what is said and confirm it in a letter to the representative. I will not give you a sample letter as I cannot believe a lawyer or conveyancer would be so foolish as to advise you about your mortgage.

Selling a home

As a general rule, people in Australia employ the services of a real estate agent to sell their homes. Private sales do occur but they are the exception to the rule. A private seller in the real estate market is treated with suspicion in a way that does not apply in other industries. People selling their motor vehicles privately and private litigants, for example, are par for the course in the used car and legal services markets. I am constantly amazed that people sign up so readily to sell their homes through real estate agents, but clearly the industry is doing something that keeps the market satisfied, otherwise people would look elsewhere to buy and sell real estate. You need to work closely with your agent, however, and one of the first things they will want is a contract for sale. Letter 12.4 may be useful.

12.4   Letter to agent

Ms Ann Agent
Principal
Hometown Real Estate
55 Commercial Road
HOMETOWN STA 23211

Dear Ms Agent,

Thank you for listing my house at 27 Household Drive, Hometown, for sale with your agency. I note you are a member of the MULTIWIDE group of agents and you will market the house through your network on an exclusive listing for three months.

As requested, I am enclosing a contract for sale prepared by my conveyancing representative Mr N. O. Worries of Ace Conveyancing Services. You will find all the certificates you need attached to the contract and I will be pleased to provide any further information you may require.

I am happy to allow you access to the house on reasonable notice for the purpose of inspections by prospective purchasers. Security is a problem, however, and access will be available only when I am at home. I trust this will not be a problem.

I wish you every success with your marketing program and once again I would like to thank you for your kind attention and professional service.

Yours sincerely,

A. Seller (Ms)

Needless to say, you will normally instruct your lawyer or conveyancer to prepare the contract for sale and perhaps you will still have some of the certificates you need from when you purchased the home. Alternatively, your council rates or water rates notice will have sufficient information to enable the conveyancing representative to begin work on the contract. Even if you have old certificates, generally they must be updated if you obtained them more than six months ago. Remember your duty of disclosure under the law—you must give proper notice of any defect or problem you know about. Instruct your lawyer or conveyancer in writing and let them work out how to express the defect or problem in the contract. Some examples of potential problems that come to mind relate to services including electricity wires, telephone cables and water and sewerage pipes. Although you may not know the extent of your duty of disclosure, the lawyer or conveyancer is supposed to know, and you have discharged your obligations once you give your conveyancing representative all the information at your disposal.

Another thing you need to think about when you are selling your house is paying out your mortgage. You will probably pay a penalty—usually one month's interest—for early repayment of the loan. If you give less than three months' notice of early repayment you will probably be slugged another fee in the form of more penalty interest. Like the church, banks get you coming in *and* going out, and you need to write to the bank as soon as you decide to sell the house. Letter 12.5 may be useful.

12.5   Letter to mortgagee

Mr Don Satrap
Lending Manager
Usury Bank
44 Railway Road
CAPITAL CORNER STA 24444

Dear Mr Satrap,

I am pleased to inform you that my house at 27 Household Drive, Hometown, is now listed for sale with Ann Agent of Hometown Real Estate. I expect the house will sell quickly and I would be obliged if you could arrange for my mortgage to be discharged.

I understand that I may be liable for one month's penalty interest for early repayment of the loan. Also, you may require a minimum of three months' notice of early repayment, otherwise further penalty interest could be payable.

Please inform me of the conditions of the loan relating to early repayment so that appropriate arrangements can be made. Would you also be kind enough to indicate any other fees payable to the bank on settlement of the loan.

You will be aware that a number of alternative housing loan products have been marketed since I took out my loan with the bank. When I take out a new loan I will be considering those products, and I understand that many of them do not include penalty interest for early repayment.

I look forward to hearing from you.

Yours sincerely,

A. Seller (Ms)

Renting a home

If you lived in West Germany, the decision to rent or buy would not be as difficult as it is in Australia. The cost of real estate in Australia always seems to be just out of reach, so people tend to rent on the basis that it is only short term and take short lease accommodation in the hope that they will soon be able to buy. In West Germany, the cost of real estate for the average person is prohibitive (as a rule of thumb, it takes two generations to pay off a house), so rental accommodation is much more stable. In Australia, we have the added problem that the turnover of property is very high and some landlords tend to think about real estate as a short term investment.

Any bargaining with your prospective landlord should be done before you sign the lease, and certainly before you move into the house. Landlords are much more amenable while their premises are vacant. Consider committing yourself to a residential lease for two years or more and you will be surprised at the concessions you might receive from a genuine landlord. If the landlord can enjoy the good life and forget about their property for two years, you are more likely to get new paint, clean carpet, the broken door fixed and two weeks' rent-free accommodation while you settle in. All you need to do is ask, and Letter 12.6 will confirm the verbal arrangements.

12.6   Letter confirming request for lease

Mr Fred Landlord
179 Coconut Drive
Whitesands Beach
PARADISE BAY STA 29299

Dear Fred,

I refer to my inspection of your premises at 27 Rent Road, Paradise Bay, and now formally request a lease for a term of two years at a weekly rental of $240. I am enclosing copies of references, which I hope you will find satisfactory. In particular, the reference from Rocket Real Estate confirms my previous lease for two years.

Prior to my taking possession of the premises, I note you will make the following repairs:

- Three broken roof tiles are to be replaced.
- Water stain on lounge room wall needs attention.
- Paint is peeling off the ceiling in the main bedroom.
- Toilet cistern is leaking and the valve should be replaced.
- Water spout in the kitchen sink needs to be fixed.
- The awning over the back porch is detached from one hinge.

I hope these repairs do not cause you any serious inconvenience. Perhaps they could be carried out during the two weeks' rent-free period you promised.

Yours sincerely,

V. G. Renter

V.G. Renter (Ms)

Dealing with the landlord's agent may be a better option than approaching the landlord. Agents are practical people and prefer to fix the repair jobs at the beginning of the lease rather than have you withholding rent or upbraiding them because the house you are renting is falling apart. In your letter to the landlord or the agent, be careful not to list every conceivable problem in the premises, as you will almost certainly go to the bottom of the renters' queue. List only those items you require repaired, and once the repairs have been done and the lease signed (and before you take possession), give the landlord or agent a separate list of all other aspects of the premises that are deficient, such as cracks in paths and walls, broken fences, damaged fittings and so on. Have the landlord or agent sign the list so you are not held responsible at the end of your lease.

For a small fee you can ask the Residential Tenancies Tribunal to resolve a dispute with your landlord. Time limits apply, and if you want to dispute a rent increase or complain about a landlord failing to repair or provide essential services, your complaint must be lodged within 30 days of the date you became aware of the problem. An extension of time may be granted in exceptional circumstances. In an urgent case such as harassment by a landlord, or where a need exists for immediate repairs, the tribunal will hear your claims within a few days. You would need to support your application for an urgent hearing with suitable documents such as a copy of a police report where harassment is a problem, or a letter from a tradesman in the case of repairs.

Usually, you would represent yourself before the Residential Tenancies Tribunal so you should attend the tribunal and find out how it works before your case is heard. You can be sure the landlord or their agent is experienced and knows the ropes so far as presenting evidence and calling witnesses is concerned. Generally, tribunal staff will assist although they will not provide legal advice. You will find your local library has one of the tenants' handbooks available in most States and Territories and these are a valuable resource for finding out how to run your case. A number of tenants' advice and advocacy services exist in capital cities and representatives from the services will advise you how to prepare your documents.

You may need to terminate your lease early due to a job in a different area or because of a change in circumstances and you can no longer afford the rent. Ideally, you will find another tenant and assign your lease, with the landlord's approval. If you cannot find another tenant you will still be responsible for the rent until the end of the term, unless the landlord agrees to cancel the lease. The landlord or their agent may find another tenant, but you will be responsible for advertising costs and any re-letting fee charged by the agent. Make sure you negotiate with the agent or landlord and write Letter 12.7 advising of your intention to vacate the premises.

12.7 Letter terminating lease

Mr Fred Landlord
179 Coconut Drive
Whitesands Beach
PARADISE BAY STA 29299

Dear Fred,

I am writing to inform you that I am obliged to break my lease on your house at 27 Rent Road, Paradise Bay, due to an illness in the family. I will be leaving the house at the end of the month and this letter is formal notice of termination of lease.

Some people I know are interested in renting the house and I have asked them to contact you. If you need to find another tenant, I ask that you arrange for advertisements to be placed in the local paper as soon as possible. I will be happy to show the house to prospective tenants.

I sincerely regret leaving as I have been very comfortable in your house. You may be willing to make some concession on the rent given that the circumstances of my leaving are beyond my control. Alternatively, you will be aware of the provisions of the Residential Tenancies Act that require a landlord to mitigate his or her loss where a tenant leaves early.

I will contact you again in a few days to arrange an inspection of the house and to organise for the keys to be handed to you or your agent. A final inspection report will need to be completed and signed when I leave.

Yours sincerely,

V. G. Renter

V. G. Renter (Ms)

Another reason for terminating a lease early would be a domestic dispute between two tenants requiring one of them to leave the premises. Normally, the person leaving would need to obtain an Apprehended Violence Order (AVO) against the remaining tenant and present a copy of the order to the landlord. Both tenants remain liable for the rent if they are parties to the lease, but the landlord can ask the remaining tenant to pay the total rent. If the landlord follows this course, the remaining tenant could seek to recover the other tenant's share of the rent as an aspect of the AVO. The court could make an order that the tenant who is forced to leave by the remaining tenant is not obliged to reimburse the remaining tenant for rent.

A generous landlord will allow a tenant to terminate their lease before the end of the term if the tenant is in difficult circumstances. You should notify the tenant in writing of your agreement to waive rent after a certain date, provided the house is left in good repair. If you decide to hold the tenant to the terms of the lease, the Residential Tenancies Act requires you to mitigate your loss, and you will be unable, for example, to recover unpaid rent if you fail to take steps to find another tenant. A landlord has the same rights as a tenant to approach the Residential Tenancies Tribunal to resolve disputes over breaches of the lease. You can also obtain an order to evict a difficult tenant who fails to remedy a breach.

Renting business premises

If you are leasing retail, commercial or industrial premises, you can afford to be a bit more demanding as the rent will generally be much higher than the rent for residential premises, and the term of your lease will generally be longer. Negotiations prior to a lease of business premises are very important, and some of the points you should cover are as follows:

- Ask for a fixed rent for the term of the lease. Most retail or commercial leases provide for annual increases in rent. The tough times for business over the past few years, however, have resulted in one good spin-off, and that is that landlords

COULD YOU TELL THEM TO LEAVE IN THE NICEST POSSIBLE WAY? BECAUSE THEY DIDN'T TAKE ANY NOTICE OF ME

are more inclined to agree to a fixed rent, perhaps with a rent review on the exercise of any option for renewal in the lease.

- Fixed rent includes such charges as a proportion of rates and taxes, maintenance and service fees for common areas, and so on. Many business leases provide that tenants are to pay a proportion of such expenses based on the area they occupy. Try to secure a rental that includes these additional charges as they can be very expensive, particularly if the building includes a lift. The least you should do if your prospective landlord will not be moved is to get a written estimate of these expenses so that you can calculate your actual rental. You may be quite shocked and find yourself looking for cheaper premises.

- Ask for as long a term as possible, perhaps five or six years. When you first go into business you may be apprehensive about a longer term, but if your business or clientele is already established, or you are purchasing an existing business, the longer the term the better. In many businesses, particularly retail businesses, without a lease you have no business. At the end of the term of the lease the landlord can put you out and carry on the business himself or, worse, sell the business to one of your competitors.

- Try for an option for a further term, as you have nothing to lose if you do not exercise it. The rental to be paid during the option period will inevitably be the subject of some negotiation. Most leases provide that the rental during the first year of the option period shall be the market rental, as determined by an independent real estate agent or independent valuer. Always choose the valuer, as valuers use well-recognised formulas to calculate market rentals. Make sure that the lease provides for the valuer to be appointed by the President of the Institute of Valuers.

Negotiations before securing a retail, commercial or industrial lease are sufficiently important to incorporate the above points in a letter to the landlord or his agent prior to the granting of a lease. Of course, you need to speak with the landlord or his agent first and find out about the demand for the premises and the kind of offer the landlord is likely to accept. A ridiculous offer will be a waste of time, but even a reasonable one will be unacceptable to some landlords who insist on calling the tune. Beware of the landlord who gets you committed to their premises and then sends you a lease full of surprises. Inevitably they will blame the solicitor or some other misfortune for the harsh terms of the lease.

On the other hand, if you have taken the initiative with a comprehensive letter, the landlord will be hard-pressed to justify any additional conditions in the lease. Another reason for sending a letter is the breathing space it gives you in case you change your mind, or find more suitable premises. A business lease is a significant commitment and I urge you to take your time. Letter 12.8 is a bold offer to your prospective landlord.

12.8 Letter to landlord

Ms H. I. Tech
General Manager
Cyberspace Industrial Village
492 Production Drive
CYBER VALLEY STA 29888

Dear Ms Tech,

I refer to my inquiries regarding a lease of Unit 7 in the Cyberspace Industrial Village and confirm I am prepared to take a lease of the premises on the following terms and conditions:

1. A lease for a term of three (3) years with an option for a further three (3) years.
2. Rent to be $1500 per month payable monthly in advance and no bond payable.
3. Rent to be fixed for the term of the lease, and the amount of rent payable in the first year of the option period is to be the agreed market rental as determined by a valuer appointed by the President for the time being of the Institute of Valuers.
4. Rent during the second year of the option period shall increase by eight (8) per cent and during the third year by ten (10) per cent.
5. All outgoings of the Industrial Village such as rates and taxes, cleaning common areas, lighting of common areas, maintenance and repairs, garbage removal and security are to be included in the rent.
6. I will bear your legal fees in connection with the preparation of the lease.

If these terms and conditions are acceptable, please arrange for your solicitor to forward a lease at your convenience.

Yours sincerely,
Fast Lane Manufacturing Company

H. I. Flyer

H. I. Flyer (Mr)
Chief Executive Officer

Whether you are renting residential or commercial premises, you can always arrange for somebody else to take over your lease if your circumstances change or your business is not doing too well. You will require the landlord's consent, but the landlord cannot withhold consent unreasonably. Provided you can demonstrate that the new tenant is reputable and they can pay the rent, you are off the hook—on the face of it, at least. Most assignments of lease carry the proviso that if the new tenant does not pay the rent or causes damage to the premises, the landlord can look to the original tenant to make good any shortfall. This problem has no answer unless you can convince the landlord to terminate your lease and give the new tenant a fresh lease. It is a practical problem, as the new tenant will be anxious to take over your lease, knowing an assigned lease is cheaper than a new one, and also that you remain ultimately responsible for the rent and upkeep of the premises.

Chapter Thirteen

Government regulators

Australian Taxation Office

Australia's 1.1 million small businesses employ 3.4 million people and represent more than 96 per cent of all businesses. Following the introduction of the GST these businesses now bear the burden of collecting tax on behalf of the government's largest regulator, the Australian Taxation Office. For a country whose national hero, Ned Kelly, is honoured as a bank robber and murderer, the government has embarked on a perilous course. Not only do we resent helping the Australian Taxation Office because of our penal colony origins, small businesses in Australia are taxed at a much higher rate than our counterparts in Great Britain or America. Speaking as the proprietor of a small business, I am reminded that personal income tax was introduced in Australia as a temporary war measure in 1916 and somebody seems to have forgotten to tell the government the war is over.

Despite the negativity we express about it, most of us are scrupulously honest about paying tax, and we go to great lengths to pillory and deride tax cheats. The recent swift action by the legal profession in New South Wales to deregister lawyers who were serial bankrupts was due entirely to the fact that the bankrupt

lawyers were avoiding their tax obligations. Similarly, few of us sympathise with the victims of tax avoidance schemes promoted by snake oil salesmen. On the other hand, tax minimisation within the tax laws is a legitimate activity in which each of us is involved in one way or another. The problem with the tax laws is their extraordinary complexity, along with the inconsistency of the Australian Taxation Office in dealing with tax minimisation schemes. Like the legal system, tax minimisation has become the playground of the rich and famous, and when ordinary people seek to take advantage of loopholes in the tax laws, the taxman seems to change the rules. Express your concerns to the commissioner and Letter 13.1 could be a useful precedent.

13.1   Letter to the Commissioner of Taxation

Mr Mick Bloggs
Commissioner of Taxation
Australian Taxation Office
PO Box 9990
CANBERRA ACT 2600

Dear Commissioner,

I am considering following the example set by the big end of town and creating jobs instead of paying personal income tax. I seek your help in this important public enterprise.

As you would know, most people need widgets at some stage of their lives, and my idea is to use my widget company to create a database of widgets on the Internet. I can float the company on the stock exchange and ask investors to buy shares on the basis of the tax deductions they receive.

Unlike some of those shonky Internet companies you might have read about, my company actually has something to sell. I have an endless supply of widgets across the country. All I need to know is what kind of widget holder someone has and where it is located and I can provide the ideal widget for the situation.

Kindly let me have a product ruling on my widget proposal. You will need a prospectus, of course, but my idea is much more viable than tea trees, emus or plantation forests. If you do issue the product ruling, I ask for your assurance to my investors that you will not do a back flip if I raise more capital than you expected.

I would also like to establish a holding company and transfer my shares in the widget company to the holding company. The shares in the holding company are to be held by a unit trust on behalf of the members of my family trust. I have another discretionary trust if the family trust looks a bit dodgy.

You may wonder about the jobs I intend creating, but I was thinking about the number of tax officers it will take to sort out the details of this proposal. If you need more help I can recommend my accountant who has just doubled his staff to help his clients cope with the GST. My accountant and I are working together to reduce unemployment.

Assuming you issue a favourable product ruling on my widget proposal, please confirm that I am no longer required to pay personal income tax.

Yours sincerely,

N. U. Stock

N. U. Stock (Ms)

Needless to say, this letter is tongue-in-cheek, but I trust you will get my drift. You can also write to the commissioner if you are dissatisfied with your income tax assessment. You must set out in detail the grounds on which you object to the assessment, and the letter must be posted or delivered to the commissioner within 60 days after the date of service of the assessment. The grounds on which you object must be explained fully in your initial objection, and you cannot add new grounds at a later date.

Deductions allowed under the general deductions provisions of the Income Tax Assessment Act include:

- part of your household expenses as home office expenses where you operate your business from home;
- occupational clothing which is necessary or peculiar to your business such as mechanic's overalls or flight attendant's uniforms;
- subscriptions to journals, newspapers and magazines, provided they relate to the production of your assessable income;
- tools of trade which are a necessary part of your business;
- travelling expenses necessarily incurred in producing income, for instance, where you travel to your client's business premises, or travel overseas to negotiate a trade contract.

Deductions not allowed under the general deductions provisions of the Income Tax Assessment Act include:

- outgoings of capital or of a capital nature such as expenditure on land, buildings and plant (repairs to buildings and depreciation on plant are deductible under other provisions of the Act);
- outgoings incurred in the production of exempt income such as income derived by a non-resident from a source outside Australia;
- outgoings of a private or domestic nature such as travel from home to work, general living expenses and expenses relating to hobbies; and

- entertainment expenses in general and even those necessarily incurred in producing income.

Of all the government regulators, the Australian Taxation Office is the most efficient and the best department with which to do business even though it is the one you would prefer most to avoid. The best advice if you strike trouble is to gather up your file and pay a visit to the office where you lodged your return. You can leave it to your accountant or legal representative if you wish, but I would always do the sorting out myself as it is much easier to get your message across personally. If your objection to the assessment fails, I would certainly recommend that any appeal to the Taxation Review Board be conducted by your lawyer or accountant.

Ombudsman

Complaints by citizens about the Commonwealth government or its agencies and departments are dealt with by a public official called the Commonwealth ombudsman. The main focus of the Commonwealth ombudsman is complaints about taxation and defence. In general, the ombudsman will decide if actions by Commonwealth government agencies and departments are unlawful, wrong, unjust or discriminatory. If, for example, the government were to make a grant to a particular group of Aboriginal people, and another community felt it was disadvantaged by the grant, or discriminated against in the process of determining the grant, a complaint could be made to the Commonwealth ombudsman. No formal procedure is required to make a complaint and no fees are charged for the ombudsman's investigation. Complaints are accepted from individuals, community groups, corporations and anybody who believes they have been disadvantaged by the actions or decisions of a Commonwealth government agency or department.

Each State and Territory has its own ombudsman, although the Commonwealth ombudsman is also the ombudsman for the Australian Capital Territory. At the State and Territory level of government, the role of the ombudsman is to investigate complaints about government agencies and departments including local councils, police and prison officers. The authority of the ombudsman does not extend to the judiciary—courts and tribunals—or parliament, including government ministers. In reality, ombudsmen lack the power to enforce their decisions, but they do look at the big picture and will often make important recommendations. For example, ombudsmen can recommend that a decision be reconsidered or that a practice or policy should be changed. Before contacting the ombudsman, however, you should write to the government department or agency you wish to complain about and express your concerns. Use Letter 13.2 as a guide.

13.2 Letter to a government department

Ms A. Bureaucrat
Director
Department of Insight
123 Wisdom Way
CAPITAL HILL STA 28555

Dear Ms Bureaucrat,

I would like to draw your attention the unsatisfactory treatment I have received at the hands of your department. It is now several days/weeks/months since the decision/ruling that [*here state the issue you are concerned about in the fewest possible words*].

While I understand the reasons for your decision/ruling, I believe you have failed to take into account/give due weight to [*describe the precise conduct by the department you want reviewed*] and as a result I have been disadvantaged.

I believe I am entitled to a review of your decision/ruling and in support of my claim I enclose the following documents [*set out in a list any documents that confirm your position*]. As a result of the review I hope you will [*here state the action you want taken to satisfy your claim*].

Please let me have your urgent response and indicate when you will be undertaking the review of my case.

Yours sincerely,

U. N. Deterred

U. N. Deterred (Ms)

Even where the government department has no intention of reviewing your case, you must write to the officer handling your file before the ombudsman will accept your complaint. My own experience of various ombudsman is they are like a brick wall unless you have exhausted all your avenues with the relevant department. If the above letter fails to achieve the review you require, you may want to write to the officer's superior and ask that the appropriate action be taken. Sometimes you will be asked to supply additional evidence or documents. Make sure you provide photocopies of sensitive material and hold on to originals. It may be frustrating to engage in futile correspondence with the department or agency, but no shortcuts exist when you are dealing with the bureaucracy. If finally you go to the ombudsman the first thing you will be asked to provide is your correspondence with the department. Letter 13.3 to the ombudsman assumes the department has finally rejected your claim.

13.3   Letter to the ombudsman

Ms O. M. Budsman
Ombudsman
108 Solomon Street
CAPITAL HILL STA 28555

Dear Ms Budsman,

I am writing about the Department of Insight and its failure to [*here state the issue you are concerned about in the fewest possible words*]. Copies of correspondence and supporting documents are enclosed.

I believe my case involves maladministration and that the department has acted maliciously/dishonestly/unfairly/incompetently in that [*describe the decision/ruling and how the department failed to properly review it*].

The department's action has disadvantaged me to the extent that [*explain the adverse consequences of the way you have been treated*]. My treatment is unfair and not supported by the facts/weight of evidence.

Please carry out the appropriate investigation as soon as possible and indicate whether you are in a position to take action against the department.

Yours sincerely,

U. N. Deterred

U. N. Deterred (Ms)

Telecommunications ombudsman

At the time of writing, the Telecommunications ombudsman is in the news, warning customers of the collapsed telephone company One.Tel to take care when switching to alternative telephone companies. This is about as savage as it gets from the 'dog and bone' consumer watchdog. After the banks, telephone companies will cause you more grief than the combined loss of your house, your job and your spouse. The only telephone sales pitch worth listening to is to give up the phone altogether and talk to your friends on a jam tin at the end of a piece of string. When it collapsed, One.Tel had 400 000 customers, and I suspect it gained most of them by selling incomprehensible contracts to vulnerable people. Nobody understood the billing system, and although I was not a One.Tel customer myself, I was sufficiently annoyed by the collapse of the company to write Letter 13.4 to the telecommunications ombudsman.

13.4 Letter to telecommunications ombudsman

Mr John Pinnock
Telecommunications Industry Ombudsman
PO Box 276 Collins Street
WEST MELBOURNE VIC 8007

Dear Mr Pinnock,

I was interested to read in the local newspaper about your warning to customers of the collapsed telephone company One.Tel to take care when transferring to alternative service providers. This is not good advice since none of the alternative telephone companies is worth two bob. I respectfully suggest you take the opportunity to help clean up the telephone industry by recommending the following measures to the government:

1. Declare all telephone service contracts unenforceable.
2. Ban door-to-door selling of telephone services to vulnerable people.
3. Announce uniform telephone service 'plans' so that consumers have the opportunity to compare one service with another.
4. Introduce a new billing system that is comprehensible and insist that all telephone service providers adopt the system.
5. Provide for dedicated Internet telephone lines at local call rates across the country to assist country people to access the Internet on the same terms as people in the city.
6. Centralise telephone account billing and inquiry departments and allow people to access their accounts on the Internet.
7. Reduce the exorbitant cost of telephone listings and arrange for listing services to be billed separately to the cost of telephone calls and equipment.

I know you have limited resources and on this basis you may be reluctant to get too involved in the One.Tel debacle. Spare a thought for Kerry Packer, however, who lost $400 million—a cool $1000 for each One.Tel customer—and ask yourself whether something could be redeemed for this disaster in the way of improved services for customers and better standards of behaviour from the telephone companies.

Yours sincerely,

Peter Breen

Banking industry ombudsman

Something quite bizarre has happened to many city banks. My local branch, for example, is no longer staffed by human beings and evolved into a wall of automatic teller machines making it look like the gaming room in my local pub. Other branches have staff on both sides of the counter urging customers to try out Internet banking. A computer person takes you through the marvels of the Net as you wait in line to be served. You key in your pin number, hit a few more keys at the direction of the computer person, and suddenly your miserable balance appears on screen. This experience is also remarkably similar to playing the pokies—except you cannot conceal your misfortunes with fruit symbols—and it prompted me to write Letter 13.5 to the banking industry ombudsman.

13.5   Letter to banking industry ombudsman

Mr Colin Neave
Banking Industry Ombudsman
GPO Box 3A
MELBOURNE VIC 3000

Dear Mr Neave,

Last month I was hijacked from a bank queue in a city branch of ABC Bank by a staff member wanting to sell me on the idea of Internet banking. I was so grateful for the attention of another human being in a bank that I gladly submitted to everything on offer and signed up for banking on the Net. It was a big mistake.

For some reason I have been unable to extract an account balance from the Internet record of my account. Each transaction is listed (and fees, of course) but no account balance. Given that I frequently sail close to the wind with my finances, you will not be surprised to learn that my account went into debit, and the bank refused to honour a cheque I had drawn. I was charged a fee of $35 by the bank, which I suspect is illegal, but that is another matter.

What concerns me is that I wrote to the boss of ABC Bank, after he recently announced a record profit for the bank, and asked if it might not be too much trouble to inform me how to extract an account balance on the Internet. I received a message on my telephone answer machine from a person named Joanne with a number to call about my letter.

For two weeks now I have been trying to get through to the number. Either I am left in a queue (like the banking chamber) or the number is engaged. Last night I finally waited for twenty minutes, only to be told that Joanne works another shift, and I should ring back. To be perfectly frank, I would not ring again if my life depended on it.

I wonder if you might be able to inform me how I can locate the balance of my account on the Internet. A copy of a printout of the account from the Internet is enclosed, and you will see that transactions are listed, but not the account balance. Any assistance you can provide will be greatly appreciated.

Yours sincerely,

Peter Breen

Other government regulators

With the exception of Commonwealth and State ombudsmen, I am not a fan of government regulators in Australia. By and large they are toothless terriers. If they do a good job they are abolished or their powers are reduced. Many people believe that a watchdog with no teeth is better than no watchdog, but I disagree. Some government watchdogs work closely with government departments in order to develop ethical behaviour in the bureaucracy. However, often they have little influence and serve only to undermine public confidence in the government. Government regulators need to be more independent and to fearlessly exercise their powers if they are to make governments accountable.

Perhaps the government regulator with the strongest teeth is the Auditor-General whose role in the democratic process is to assist the parliament hold the executive arm of government accountable for its use of public resources. A recent Auditor-General's report to the New South Wales parliament, for example, drew attention to a document titled 'Cultural development policy' on the website of the Minister for Arts. The report found that public funds had been used for private political interests to the extent that the document promoted the aspirations of the Labor Party. As a result of the report the document was removed from the Arts Ministry website. Another function of the Auditor-General is to investigate allegations of serious and substantial waste of public money under 'whistle-blower' legislation. General powers also allow the Auditor-General to check whether a government department or agency has paid reasonable prices for its resources and applied those resources efficiently and according to the law.

As well as regulating governments, a number of Commonwealth and State bodies regulate various private sector activities. One at the Commonwealth level of government is the private health

TANDBERG

insurance ombudsman who deals with disputes involving members of health funds, doctors, dentists, hospitals and the funds themselves. Most disputes relate to the 30 per cent government rebate for private health insurance and the cost of medical and dental treatment. Private health funds are in the business of making a profit and for many people insurance premiums for routine medical and dental treatment are not good value for money when you compare the cost of these services with the rebates payable by the health funds. The ombudsman has no real answer to this problem. Similarly, the introduction of so-called lifetime health cover and no-gap medical insurance schemes raises fundamental questions for consumers that the ombudsman is unlikely to address in his role as an industry regulator.

An example of a State regulator is the energy and water ombudsman who resolves disputes on behalf of consumers of gas, electricity and water. Generally, the ombudsman works with a council consisting of industry representatives, consumers and small business interests. Theoretically, the ombudsman is independent of all those interests and government, but in the end a decision of the ombudsman will have little consequence for consumers because it has no binding force. Some consumers will be left with the feeling that they have simply been dealing with another agency of government. Serious transgressions of the rights of consumers and the public interest can occur right under the nose of government watchdogs such as the energy and water ombudsman as a recent incident dramatically demonstrated.

One member of the energy and water ombudsman scheme in New South Wales, electricity supplier TransGrid, cleared a 35-kilometre strip of forest in three national parks to prevent disruptions to electricity supply in high-voltage power lines. The work devastated the national parks and was done without proper supervision or apparent understanding of the environmental impact of large-scale forest degradation. According to newspaper reports of the incident, the Transgrid officials responsible for the work had undergone environmental training only in the previous twelve months. In this case the ombudsman appeared to have no authority to act against one of its members for environmental vandalism because the damaging activity did not occur on private property. You might wonder about the usefulness of a public watchdog that only has the power to intervene in a dispute where private interests are involved.

Other government regulators in New South Wales include the Independent Commission Against Corruption (ICAC) and the Police Integrity Commission (PIC). The former body investigates allegations of corruption against public officials and agencies. Corrupt conduct involves the dishonest or biased use of a position by a public official or public authority. Anti-corruption bodies in other States and Territories include Queensland's Criminal Justice Commission and the Anti-Corruption Commission in Western Australia. Where the allegations relate to a police officer, the PIC has a similar brief to the ICAC. Both bodies have powers comparable to those of a royal commission. The PIC was set up following a recommendation of the Royal Commission into the NSW Police Service and it plays an active role in a number of police activities including the management of telephone intercepts.

As a solicitor in private practice when the first edition of this book was published, I became aware that my telephone was tapped when I took on a defamation case for the late Bill Sinclair who was described by the *Sydney Morning Herald* as a convicted drug smuggler. In fact, Sinclair had fled Bangkok on bail and had been convicted of nothing. These days, telephone taps are much more sophisticated and officers of the PIC can listen to what you have to say on the telephone without leaving their city offices. In the 1980s the police had to go through the telephone exchange, which accounted for the interference you often heard on the line. Today, you would never know if the PIC is listening to your telephone conversations. I recently asked the police minister if it is true that New South Wales has more telephone intercepts than the whole of the United States. So far I have not received an answer.

Complaints about discrimination are dealt with by State and Territory legislation. In New South Wales the Anti-Discrimination Act prohibits discrimination based on sex, sexuality, race, marital status, age and disability. The Anti-Discrimination Board deals with complaints and seeks to resolve disputes by conciliation. If that process fails, a dispute may be referred to the Equal Opportunity Tribunal, which has the power to make a binding decision and order payment of compensation. For complaints about discrimination under Commonwealth law, the Human Rights and Equal Opportunity Commission (HREOC) is represented in each State and Territory. Determinations by HREOC are not binding, but where a person does not comply with the determination, you can ask the Federal Court to hear the complaint and make a binding order.

By far the most important government regulator is the Federal and State courts system. Judges too are part of the government, although their independence from the legislature and the executive arm of government is guaranteed by Chapter Three of the Australian Constitution. The problem with the courts is demonstrated by the fact that access to the other government regulators I have mentioned is free while justice is likely to cost you an arm and a leg. Lawyers inevitably get the blame for the cost of justice, but the real problem is the complexity of laws, and this is the responsibility of government. Statutes are written in convoluted language that often makes no sense and laws overlap in a way that few people can follow. Judges are left to make difficult decisions that are often seen as arbitrary, inconsistent and late. Governments attack the symptoms of the problem—lawyers and the courts—while acts of parliament are piled one on top of the other in the legislatures for the casual scrutiny of the privileged and the pedantic.

Populist governments in Australia also pillory lawyers and the courts in order to promote their law and order agendas. This is a cynical appeal to the middle class constituencies both major parties represent. Law and order demands more power for police and less tolerance by the courts. The convenience of populism is its appeal to the left and right of the political spectrum. While the right emphasises strong leadership, the left demands popular equality, and the two streams of political thought seem to have converged in their opposition to traditional civil liberties, which protect minorities and the disadvantaged. In this highly charged political environment you can expect to be labelled a 'bleeding heart' if you attempt to argue the case for enforcement of individual liberties by the courts. To my mind, however, protection of basic human rights and freedoms ought to be the primary focus of the courts. If judges fail to promote their courts as accessible forums for

challenging abuses of power—effective government regulators—
they will continue to serve as the whipping posts of populist
governments, and ultimately be responsible for their own demise.

Professional regulatory bodies

Just as government departments and agencies are answerable
to their regulators, the private sector is also bound to observe
certain standards of conduct and accountability. The conduct
required of individuals and corporations in the private sector
is usually determined by a combination of statutory responsibility
to the relevant minister and self-regulation. It is not possible
here to deal with every regulatory authority in every industry,
but earlier we looked briefly at regulation of the advertising
industry by the Advertising Standards Bureau and regulation
of the insurance industry in the face of the HIH Insurance
Company collapse. Here we will look at the regulation of
lawyers and doctors, and note in passing that every professional
body has some kind of regulatory regime that requires members
to comply with statutory rules about professional conduct.
Doctors and lawyers are unusual in this context because the
regulatory authority has a dual role to protect the public interest,
and also to set the standards of conduct required of the
professional.

If you were to complain about a medical practitioner you
would direct your complaint to the Health Care Complaints
Commission (HCCC). New South Wales has a Joint Parliamentary Committee that monitors and reviews the functions of the
HCCC, but ultimately the minister for health is responsible for
the way the organisation deals with your complaint. The same
minister is responsible for the Medical Board that maintains a
register of medical practitioners. A doctor cannot practise without
a licence from the Medical Board, and yet the board exercises

a considerable influence on the HCCC and the Medical Tribunal that eventually hears and determines your complaint. In fact, a member of the board sits on the tribunal. The right to be heard and the right to an independent tribunal are principles of procedural fairness (natural justice) frequently denied to medical practitioners who fall out of favour with the medical profession regulators.

The regulatory system for dealing with complaints about lawyers is no less convoluted than the doctor's watchdogs, and from the point of view of the lawyers, no less unjust. A complaint about a lawyer would normally go to the legal services ombudsman (in New South Wales he or she is called the legal services commissioner) and the ombudsman would carry out an initial inquiry before deciding whether the professional bodies—the Bar Association and the Law Society—should become involved in the investigation. If questions arise about trust moneys, or allegations are made involving serious misconduct, the ombudsman would normally involve the professional bodies in the inquiries. This immediately raises a conflict for the professional bodies who are supposed to be the lawyers' trade unions. At least doctors have separate trade union representation to the regulatory regime.

Another conflict for the legal profession is that the regulators are funded by the same lawyers they are supposed to be investigating. Lawyers who step out of line often complain that the professional bodies can be extremely difficult and unhelpful, as if they need to demonstrate their lack of bias towards the lawyers. Frequently I am asked to intervene on behalf of lawyers who are having trouble with the regulators and I am constantly amazed that the regulators seem to make a huge fuss over comparatively minor matters while appearing to ignore more serious complaints.

As a consumer, you may take a different view to the one I have expressed and be heartened by the high standards required of doctors and lawyers by the professional regulatory bodies.

In fact, they are double standards, particularly if the professional person has acted negligently. Lawyers in New South Wales operate their own professional indemnity insurance scheme and yet no independent system exists to advise you of your right to sue for negligence. Once I visited the Law Society about a negligence claim against a group of solicitors and I was shocked to find one of the solicitors in the group working behind the society's inquiry counter. Similarly, doctors are represented by a professional indemnity insurer who will defend to the death any negligence claim you might want to make against your doctor. For years I have been complaining about the raw deal consumers receive from these regulatory bodies and the difficulties involved in suing doctors and lawyers for negligence.

Chapter Fourteen

Employment

Unfair dismissal

Once I believed it was unnecessary to give employees written warnings (or any warning for that matter) before you dismiss them. Then a friend of mine, a small business operator, was the victim of a serial claimant for unfair dismissal, and I was obliged to think again about warnings to unsatisfactory employees. Under State and Commonwealth law, a dismissal is unfair if it is harsh, unjust or unreasonable. If the dismissed employee takes their case to the Industrial Relations Commission (IRC), a number of aspects to the dismissal will be considered in deciding what is unfair. Whether or not you gave an employee a warning will be an important aspect of the claim, although the real question is whether a valid reason for the dismissal existed. For example, you may be able to show that the employee was stealing from you, or providing trade information to your competitors. Clearly, you would not be required to give a warning in these circumstances.

Since my friend's case I would always give a written warning to an unsatisfactory employee. The lawyer for my friend advised him to settle on the doorstep of the IRC for $20 000. My friend told the sacked employee (who had apparently made three previous claims for unfair dismissal) and the lawyer he did not have $20 000. The employee settled for my friend's car, a late model Holden Commodore. Registration papers were signed over on the spot, the keys were handed to the employee and my friend caught a taxi home. According to the lawyer, the outcome might have been different if my friend had given the employee a written warning prior to the dismissal notice. I am now reliably informed that best practice demands three warnings to an unsatisfactory employee over a period not exceeding six months, and at least one of the warnings should be in writing.

The average IRC award in the electrical trades industry, for example, is ten weeks' pay, with a maximum award of six months' pay. Apart from awarding compensation, the IRC can order reinstatement to a former position or re-employment in another position. Most cases are resolved by conciliation with the parties signing mutual releases without admission of liability. Provisions requiring confidentiality are frequently included in a release. If conciliation fails to resolve a claim it will be referred to arbitration. The IRC is not bound by the rules of evidence, and usually the parties are required to bear their own costs, except where a claim is frivolous or vexatious, or where the unsuccessful party fails to agree to a reasonable offer to settle the claim. If you are dissatisfied with a decision of the IRC you can appeal within 21 days provided you have leave of the full bench comprising three or more members or judges.

It is always difficult to know the best way to inform an employee that their performance is not up to scratch. Very good managers are able to introduce employees to new technology or new responsibilities in such a way that the employee embraces the task as a challenge, or as an extension of their skills. Others have a more direct approach. In collecting the material for this book, I interviewed the personnel manager of an international computer company in Melbourne. I was astounded to find that the company had a standard letter for employees whose performances were unsatisfactory, and the latest recipient of the letter had been no less an employee than the Victorian general manager. Letter 14.1 is the computer company's warning letter.

14.1   Warning letter to manager

CONFIDENTIAL

Mr U. R. Belowpar
General Manager
Clear View Computer Company
24 Ambulatory Way
NEW HEIGHTS STA 24711

Dear Mr Belowpar,

As discussed at the board meeting last week, we are not satisfied with your performance as general manager of the company. Profits continue to decline, and we no longer enjoy a major share of the Australian market.

Although we realise that some of the results may be due to matters beyond your control, you have indicated that certain personal problems are contributing to your deteriorated performance. While we sympathise with these personal problems, you must realise that we require a fully operational person in your position.

Since you have now had two verbal warnings, we advise that if your performance does not dramatically improve within the next four (4) weeks, we will be forced to take steps to terminate your employment.

Yours sincerely,
Clear View Computer Company

I. M. Warning

I. M. Warning
Chairman of Directors

Generally you can assume that a warning will be more important in the case of an employee whose termination relates to unsatisfactory work performance. You can dismiss the employee summarily if you wish, but justice demands that you give the person an opportunity to improve their performance. In fact, the Commonwealth unfair dismissal laws, which are supervised by the Australian Industrial Relations Commission (AIRC), provide that the commission must have regard to whether the employee had been warned about unsatisfactory work performance where that is an issue in the termination. As with State unfair dismissal laws, the federal legislation does not specify how many warnings should be given, but the warning prior to dismissal should indicate the conduct or behaviour that needs to improve. Personally, I would put the warning in writing even though it is not compulsory, and Letter 14.2 may be a useful guide.

14.2 Warning letter to assistant

Ms Kay Ottic
Personnel Assistant
Ace Personnel Services
126 Performance Drive
NEW HEIGHTS STA 24711

Dear Kay,

I asked you to rearrange the client filing system and now I am unable to find any files. Each of the four drawers in the filing cabinet is neat as a pin, but I cannot work out how the files are grouped. Please explain the system to me and then label the drawers.

Other files are piled on your desk, stacked on the floor and falling out of your bookcase. If you need another filing cabinet, let me know, otherwise the only files floating around your office should be the ones you are working on.

I am also concerned that you seem to attend to those files you are interested in while other files are being neglected. Several clients have complained to me that you are not dealing with their files, and it is glaringly obvious to me that the files you ignore relate to the jobs you consider are located on the wrong side of the city.

In summary, I have been unable to detect any management plan in your work flow. Everything seems to turn into a last minute crisis. If you approached your work in a more organised fashion you would not have so many dramas, in my opinion.

Finally, I would like to say you are employed to work a 40-hour week. You always seem to be engaged in your social and private activities whenever I pass your desk and you happen to be on the telephone. This drives me crazy, along with the number of days you arrive late, leave early and ring in sick.

I regret to say that unless your performance dramatically improves I will have no alternative but to take steps to terminate your employment.

Yours sincerely,
Ace Personnel Services

Elle Liminator.

Elle Liminator
General Manager

Commonwealth industrial law distinguishes between unfair and unlawful terminations. A termination is unlawful if you dismiss an employee for temporary absence from work because of illness or injury; taking part in trade union activities; participating in legal proceedings or representing employees; refusing to sign or negotiate an Australian Workplace Agreement; absence from work during parental leave; and various grounds of discrimination including age, race, sex, sexual preference, marital status, social origins, family responsibilities, physical or mental disability, and the list goes on. An employee must choose whether to commence proceedings in the Federal Court for unlawful termination or lodge a claim in the AIRC. Most claims would be lodged in the commission for reasons of cost and simplicity of proceedings. State law also covers illegal dismissals for pregnancy, unlawful discrimination, complaints about workplace health and safety, union membership and dismissal within six months of a workplace

injury. Where a dismissal is illegal as opposed to unfair, you may be sued for damages or other relief. You may also be liable to prosecution by government inspectors and unions.

Many employers attempt to avoid unfair dismissal laws by engaging employees under a contract of employment for a fixed term of six months or less. These contracts are frequently expressed to be renewable every six months, but they do not achieve their purpose of defeating the unfair dismissal laws. Generally, they are not regarded as contracts for a specified period or specified task, and they will be struck down in any event if the employee can demonstrate that you insisted on a contract just to avoid unfair dismissal laws. Another possibility is that employers will engage employees on a casual basis to circumvent the unfair dismissal regime, but this scheme will fail if the employee has worked for you on a regular and systematic basis for twelve months or more and the employee had a reasonable expectation that the job would continue. You can engage an employee for a qualifying or probationary period, but the maximum period is three months. After three months the unfair dismissal laws apply and you are deemed to have an employment contract with your employee. In fact, all employees have contracts —whether they are written or oral—and it is good practice to confirm an employee's appointment in writing as your letter will then become an effective written contract. Letter 14.3 may assist.

14.3   Letter confirming appointment

Mr N. U. Staffer
Production Assistant
Newline Manufacturing Company
99 Progress Drive
NEW HEIGHTS STA 24711

Dear Mr Staffer,

We are pleased to confirm your appointment as Production Assistant in our Assembly Department, effective from 6 July. Your salary will be $50 000 per annum paid fortnightly into your bank account.

As discussed during our interview, your duties include [*state duties in full*].

Conditions of your employment are based on a working week of 40 hours, and actual office hours are 9.00 a.m. to 5.00 p.m. Monday to Friday, with a rostered day off every fourth week. Annual leave granted is twenty (20) working days.

After a qualifying period of six months you will be eligible to join our staff contributory Superannuation Plan.

Your employment is on a [*state whether permanent, temporary or fixed term*] basis and is terminable by either party giving two weeks' notice in writing.

Kindly acknowledge your acceptance of the above conditions by signing and returning the attached copy of this letter.

We look forward to working together for our mutual benefit.

Yours sincerely,
Newline Manufacturing Company

W. Vision

W. Vision (Ms)
Personnel Manager

Independent contractors

An important question for all employers is whether the contract you have with your employee is a contract of employment or a services contract. Employment contracts are covered by award conditions and your contractual relationship is governed by State and Commonwealth law in relation to sick pay, holiday pay, superannuation, long service leave and so on. You cannot avoid your statutory obligations even when you enter a workplace agreement with your employees. A workplace agreement must pass the 'no disadvantage' test, which means the wages and conditions must not be less than the relevant award. The effect of the workplace agreement is to override the award for the term of the agreement. A contract of services, on the other hand, is not a relationship between employer and employee for the purposes of industrial law, and award conditions do not apply to the relationship. Rather, the person you engage is an independent or sub-contractor, and you may wish to confirm their contract in writing using Letter 14.4 as a starting point.

14.4   Letter to independent contractor

Mr U. R. Lonestar
General Contractor
Manufacturing Assistance Company
21 Independence Drive
NEW HEIGHTS STA 24711

Dear Mr Lonestar,

We are pleased to confirm your contract to supply widgets for our new range of steel posts. You will receive $120 per widget including GST.

Design of the widgets is your responsibility although the design should meet our performance standards as noted in the specifications accompanying your tender. You are responsible for any injury or damage sustained as a result of defective widgets.

You are free to use our premises for the manufacture of the widgets. We will supply the space you need in our factory, but you must provide your own materials and tools. We can arrange for you to lease a steel-turning lathe.

So long as you supply the widgets as we need them you are free to set your own hours and work conditions. We understand you have insurance for public liability and workers' compensation to cover your two assistants.

It is not possible to estimate demand for the steel posts. Like any new product range, some initial buyer resistance can be expected. Long-term, however, we anticipate securing a good share of the market, based on our experience in the United Kingdom.

We are committed to producing 10 000 steel posts, and on this basis we can assure you of work for the next twelve (12) months. After that production will be driven by demand and you will need to make your own assessment of the situation.

If these conditions are acceptable please sign and return the attached copy of this letter no later than next Monday and you need to be ready to start work the following Monday.

Yours sincerely,
Newline Manufacturing Company

Amelia Rate

Amelia Rate
General Manager

Personally I am not mad about this letter because the status of the contractor is not as clear as it may seem. Whenever you bring a contractor onto your premises to manufacture goods or perform a service contract, questions arise about their independence, and the questions are not always easy to answer. With the best will in the world you can find yourself in the relationship of employer and employee when you actually intended something more informal. Also, since the introduction of the GST, an independent or sub-contractor needs an Australian Business Number (ABN) from the tax office otherwise you must retain 48.5 per cent of your payments to the contractor for withholding tax. If possible, have the contractor work outside your premises and make sure they make their own insurance arrangements. As an employer, you bear the onus of proving a person is not an employee.

Other factors to be taken into account when deciding whether a person is an employee include the nature of the job, whether you are paying the person on a regular basis, whether you are providing materials and setting work conditions, and the expectations the person has for ongoing work. You will no doubt prefer the independent or sub-contractor arrangement to the contract of employment because you will not be responsible for such things as payment of workers' compensation insurance, deducting tax instalments and so on. If you have a written contract of services with an independent or sub-contractor it will not be conclusive evidence of anything except your intention at the time the contract was signed.

Applications for employment

When you advertise a job and fill the position, inevitably you will disappoint some applicants who may have been perfectly suitable employees. The needs of your business and the people for whom you are directly responsible, however, are somehow more immediate than a stranger looking for employment. It is important nevertheless to communicate to the disappointed applicants, who need to be encouraged in their search for work. Young people, in particular, with limited experience and boundless dreams ought to have the benefit of your reassurance about their prospects. Also, the person you select for the job may not work out and, just in case, you will want to remain on good terms with those job applicants who were unsuccessful. Letter 14.5 may be a helpful guide.

14.5   Employer's letter declining job application

Mr V. G. Credentials
63 Opportunity Avenue
NEW HEIGHTS STA 24711

Dear Mr Credentials,

Thank you for your letter applying for the position of Manager's Assistant and for sending us a copy of your résumé. We received a surprisingly large number of applications for this position, which made the choice of applicants to invite for an interview very difficult.

We regret to inform you that your application has not been successful. We do thank you for your interest in Clear View Computer Company, however, and wish you success in obtaining employment suitable to your qualifications.

May we take this opportunity to compliment you on your qualifications and your excellent résumé. If a suitable position becomes available we will contact you.

Yours sincerely,
Clear View Computer Company

W. Vision

W. Vision (Ms)
Personnel Manager

Searching for a job is no fun, particularly if it is your first job, or you have lost a previous job. The task has been made more difficult by the proliferation of casual work and the decreasing influence of the union movement in the labour market. More jobs are won through friends and acquaintances than are likely to appear in the employment pages of the newspaper. If you are willing to travel, your chances of getting a job will improve, and it is worth remembering that the Australian workforce was built on the backs of migrants who left family, home and country to find work.

The first thing you need to know when you find the job you want is the form of job application needed. You will want to get off to the right start and the way you apply for the job is crucial. A letter in response to an advertisement for a job should tell your prospective employer the following:

1. *How you know about the job.* You may have seen the advertisement in the press, been informed by an employment agency or heard about it from a friend. Perhaps you found the job on the Internet.
2. *Your qualifications for the job.* Your prospective employer will want to know about your education, training and experience, as well as any awards you might have won or other formal recognition of your work.
3. *Your ability to do the job.* It is important to tell your prospective employer why you think you can do the job, but be careful not to exaggerate your talents. Include references with your application, or promise to forward them prior to an interview.
4. *Contact point.* Tell your prospective employer how to get in touch with you to arrange an interview. A telephone contact is essential.

In my experience, a prospective employer will want a brief letter accompanied by a separate résumé/curriculum vitae setting out your relevant personal information. If you include everything the employer might need in the letter, it will be too long and boring. A résumé allows you to set out your qualifications and experience in an orderly fashion. Your letter should deal briefly with the four points listed above and it should be painstakingly impersonal to minimise the chances of your prospective employer making a decision based on some personality trait conveyed in the way you write. Letter 14.6 may be helpful.

14.6   Job application and résumé

Mr N. O. Detention
Migrant Adviser
Independent Migration Advisory Service
128 Precedent Parade
NEW HEIGHTS STA 24711

Dear Mr Detention,

I refer to your advertisement in the *Voice* on Saturday 6 July, for a migration adviser.

I worked for the Department of Immigration and Multicultural Affairs at the Australian Consulate in New York between August and October 1999. This experience prompted my interest in migration and multicultural affairs and I am currently undertaking a diploma course in migration services at Melbourne University.

I am enclosing a list of personal details. Should my qualifications and experience interest you I would be grateful for the opportunity of an interview. You may contact me during business hours on 8765 4321 and I look forward to hearing from you.

Yours sincerely,

Mary Jones

Mary Jones

Curriculum Vitae

Personal details

Name: Mary Jones
Address: 3 Jones Crescent, Jones Island, NSW 2430
Telephone: (02) 8765 4321
Facsimile: (02) 8765 4322
email: maryjones@ozemail.com.au
Date of birth: 12 December 1973
Interests: Travelling, bush walking, music and Irish dancing

Academic record

Tertiary education

February 1998:   Admitted as a legal practitioner in New South Wales

May–July 1997:   College of Law, St Leonards—Graduate Diploma in Legal Practice

1993–1997:   University of Sydney/Legal Practitioners Admission Board—Diploma in Law

1991–1992:   University of New South Wales—Bachelor of Social Work
                 (completed first year)

Secondary education

1990–1991:   Higher School Certificate
                 Our Lady of Mercy College, Jones Island

Work history

May–October 2000:   Travel within Europe, Middle East
                         and North America
August 1999–April 2000: Senior Clerical Officer
                         Australian Consulate, New York

Responsibilities/duties:

1. Working with the Army Adviser (October 1999–April 2000). Liaising with foreign military attachés, staff from a variety of embassies and the USA Defence Department. Researching policy issues and disseminating information on Australian Defence Force policies. Liaising with public affairs and consulate staff. Assisting with the organisation of defence functions, and managing the adviser's budget.
2. Working for the Department of Immigration and Multicultural Affairs (August–October 1999). Assessing military personnel for visas pertaining to UN operations in East Timor and general applications for visas. Liaising with USA Defence Department and the general public. Gaining knowledge of protocols for visas.

Work history *(continued)*

April–July 1999:   Travel within Europe and Australia
November 1998–April 1999: Legal Executive
                                        British Petroleum Limited, London

Responsibilities/duties:

Having conduct of and assisting in the conduct of:

- contract matters (Sale of Goods Act);
- insurance cases (personal injury and property damage claims);
- employment and corporate litigation.

Providing advice on liability and quantum to engineering staff and the insurance department, briefing counsel and instructing at hearings, preparing lists of documents, drafting answers to interrogatories and preparing defences and witness statements.

August–October 1998:   Travel across Canada
May 1996–July 1998:   Legal Clerk and Solicitor
                                        Slaughter and May, Sydney

Responsibilities/duties:

Having conduct of and assisting in the conduct of:

- personal injury and workers compensation;
- family and criminal law;
- industrial and immigration law;
- Court of Appeal cases (mainly Statute of Limitation matters).

Briefing and instructing Counsel, court appearances, liaising with appropriate experts both medical and non-medical, taking initial instructions from clients, providing advice to clients (written and oral) and drafting pleadings.

February 1995–February 1996: Legal Clerk
                                        Access Community Law Centre, Sydney

Responsibilities/duties:

General casework to prepare personal injury, workers' compensation, industrial and medical negligence cases for litigation, and instructing Counsel.

May–December 1994:   Legal Assistant
                                        Law Research Institute, Sydney

Responsibilities/duties:

Law library research, general casework and attending conferences with counsel.

Referees will be provided upon request.

If you have a particular shortcoming in your qualifications or experience, you should not ignore it in your job application. Rather, you would do well to deal with the problem in your letter and explain what you have done to overcome the shortcoming. In the present case, Mary Jones ought to have qualifications as a migration agent if she hopes to secure a job with a migration advisory service, and her letter addresses the situation with the information that she is attending the relevant course of study. It may be stating the obvious, but you need to demonstrate to a prospective employer that you are keen to develop your skills.

As a bare minimum you need to keep in touch with computer technology in your trade or industry. Most employers will expect you to know something about the computer programs that monitor and run their businesses. The Internet is also important for many businesses and you will improve your chances of getting a job if you know how to set up and manage a website. Basic skills are note difficult to acquire—the days are gone when you needed to learn HTML. A program such as Dreamweaver, for example, makes website design and production easy.

Resigning from a job

In general it is best not to leave one job until you have found another, unless, for example, you have made alternative arrangements to pay the rent, or you have a particular skill that employers will fall over each other to acquire. If you are simply dropping out of the workforce for a while, remember that returning to work is likely to be much more difficult than leaving, so avoid making an enemy of your former boss. Keep your letter of resignation simple, although you should always give your reasons for resigning. Letters 14.7 to 14.10 cover various situations and may give you some ideas.

14.7 Resignation letter A

I give notice that I shall be leaving your employment on 1 July in order to undertake an extended overseas trip. I have enjoyed working for you and I shall miss the many friends I have made in the company.

14.8 Resignation letter B

I give notice that I shall be leaving your employment on 1 July. It has been most interesting working for you, and I have learned a great deal from your company. I have found another position, however, where I shall have more opportunity to act on my own initiative, and where my chances of promotion are greater.

14.9 Resignation letter C

I regret that I must give notice and I shall be leaving at the end of the month. I shall miss the many friends I have made in the company, but I have been offered a job with shorter hours where the work is more clearly defined, which I feel will be more suitable.

14.10 Resignation letter D

For the past several months I have been carrying out my duties as secretary of the Tigers Community Association with considerable difficulty as my business commitments have been making it increasingly difficult for me to attend meetings.

In the circumstances I am unable to continue in my present active role with the Association and therefore I resign my position effective from our next monthly meeting.

I shall continue to take an interest in the Association and to provide whatever assistance I can to the new secretary.

When you resign from your job bear in mind that you have a contract with your employer and it is not unheard of for an employee to be sued at common law for wrongful termination of the employment contract. An employer may, for example, refuse to accept your notice of resignation, and argue that you have an obligation to perform your work until the contract is lawfully terminated. The employer may also attempt to withhold wages to offset damages suffered as a result of your failure to properly terminate the contract. Your contract may also provide that you cannot work for other employers during the currency of your employment and a difficult employer might claim to a court that you are not entitled to work elsewhere while the contract remains enforceable.

Dealing with a dismissal notice

Receiving a dismissal notice will be a shock to the system if you believed you had a secure job and you were performing your part of the employment contract. If you feel that the dismissal was unfair or unjust, and you earn more than about $70 000 per annum, you will not have access to the statutory unfair dismissal laws described earlier in this chapter. The appropriate remedy in those circumstances will be a claim for wrongful dismissal at common law. You would not follow this course, however, unless you were prepared to sit around until the litigation is resolved— and it may take years. In any event, a rule of common law exists to the effect that if employers cannot seek specific performance of an employment contract, then neither should employees be able to do so. Subject to getting advice in your particular circumstances about unfair dismissal, Letter 14.11 may be a good way to sign off.

14.11   Response to dismissal notice

Mr Cocky Boss
General Manager
Tunnel View Construction Company
44 Unreasonable Drive
NEW HEIGHTS STA 24711

Dear Cocky,

Thank you for the dismissal notice and your cheque for two weeks' pay in lieu of the usual notice. I am also entitled to holiday pay and long service leave and I look forward to receiving your cheque for the additional amount due.

You will be aware that underpayment of wages is an offence under industrial law and the debt can be recovered in the relevant court together with interest and costs.

I enjoyed working for you and regret you did not appreciate my services. If you need my advice or assistance in the future please let me know.

Yours sincerely,

Q. Wit (Ms)

Avoid being offensive, defamatory or threatening in your response to a dismissal notice, but you can afford to be impertinent

if you feel the need. Say something complimentary if possible, such as recognition of your former employer as a market leader, as that will hurt more than any number of insults. If you are depressed or angry do not write a letter; instead, ask a friend to do it for you. You might also seek professional assistance—I have known people to spend years getting over the loss of a job because they felt the need to tough it out on their own when appropriate counselling might have given them a new perspective on their situation in just a few weeks. Above all, get yourself into a frame of mind where you are thinking about the next job and not the last one. It may not be easy. If ever you had your employment unexpectedly terminated you will not be surprised to learn that losing a job is second only to divorce in the causes of stress-related illnesses.

Seeking a pay rise

Always ask for a pay rise if you think you are worth it. Most employers would prefer to pay you more money than have you work at half pace because you are unhappy with your salary. You should be guided by the salaries received by other people in your industry doing similar work to you, and you should be forthright in your request. Personally I would try approaching my employer on an informal basis before writing a letter for a pay rise. If the boss is unhappy with some aspect of your work you can be sure they will take the opportunity to let you know you have a problem. And make sure you pick the right moment. Avoid asking for a pay rise when the boss has a pressing matter to deal with, for example. An informal request for a pay rise may not bear fruit immediately, but it could result in a clear statement of what you need to achieve to earn the extra money. Try Letter 14.12 if the informal approach is not working.

14.12   Letter requesting pay rise

Mr Cocky Boss
General Manager
Tunnel View Construction Company
44 Unreasonable Drive
NEW HEIGHTS STA 24711

Dear Cocky,

I have been hoping to discuss my salary for the past few weeks, but we have been so busy that the time never seems right to approach you.

At the commencement of my employment you indicated you would review my salary after twelve (12) months if I assumed full responsibility for my department. The period of twelve (12) months has elapsed and the department has been autonomous now for three months.

I feel that my added responsibility and the increased profitability and independence of the department are such that an increase in salary is reasonable.

I hope you are in a position to consider my request favourably.

Yours sincerely,

S. Tay

S. Tay (Ms)

A request for a pay rise will often be the result of a change in duties or work conditions you did not anticipate when you took on the job. Like any contract, a contract of employment cannot be unilaterally varied, and your boss is not entitled to require you to work in a particular place or under certain conditions unless the variation is implied in your contract. You should be paid any work expenses you incur as a result of minor variations to the work contract, but major variations may amount to termination. If you were employed to do a job indoors, for example, and your employer suddenly decides you must work in the open, this could effectively terminate your employment contract and you would be entitled to recover damages.

If you are paid above award wages and your employer fails to pay you increases in the award, this is not a breach of your employment contract unless a percentage increase in line with rises in the award was agreed to—preferably before you started work. You can work for reduced wages under protest for a short time without losing your right to sue for damages. Attempts to force wage reductions on employees or to remove entitlements such as a motor vehicle are not common in Australia. More important is your right to wages and entitlements where your employer goes into liquidation. This is an issue that governments in Australia have failed to satisfactorily address.

Chapter Fifteen

Business and personal letters

Reference letters

I have just been asked by an old friend for a reference in support of a job application with the Northern Territory government. When I asked my friend if I could use the reference in *The Book of Letters* he replied, 'Heavens no! If people in Canberra find out I am working for the Territory government it is likely to lose its funding.' Immediately I was challenged to write a reference in such precise terms that nobody could possibly accuse me of misleading my friend's prospective employer. Letter 15.1 is the result.

15.1   Personal reference letter

To whom it may concern

I have known John Smith for the past 30 years and he is a good friend. He has performed a number of political tasks for me over the years and has assisted me in election campaigns. On several occasions I have engaged him as an unpaid adviser. He has worked in a salaried capacity for other members of parliament who will no doubt vouch for his work skills.

As a friend I can say that John enjoys my complete confidence. I value his political acumen and judgment and I often seek his opinion about current political issues. His knowledge and experience of Australian politics guarantees an accurate assessment of the affairs of the day.

Of course, John is absolutely trustworthy in financial matters and he understands the need for confidentiality and diplomacy in sensitive situations. I regard him as a trusted adviser and personal confidant and I can only assume he undertakes his professional work with the same diligence and integrity with which he conducts his private affairs.

John is good company and a congenial host. He has a wide circle of friends as well as a loving family. I have no hesitation in recommending him for a position involving political analysis and research. I emphasise, however, that John has undertaken such work for me as a friend on a voluntary basis.

Yours sincerely,

Peter Breen

As you might have gathered I do not want to be responsible for skeletons in my friend's political cupboard, although I would like to help him get a job. I have therefore taken care to limit the reference to my personal experience, which is quite different from a professional employment relationship. It may sound callous, but singing the praises of a friend in a reference letter without limiting your remarks to your own personal experience is a bit like signing up to go to war—war in the courts. I always take care in a personal reference letter and make sure my remarks can be used only to assess the personal character of the person I am recommending, particularly when I know that the letter will be used to support a job application.

Taking care with the details is a good rule to follow whenever you are asked to write a reference letter. The rule is especially important in the case of a business reference for an ex-employee or colleague. At common law you can be responsible for the consequences if you say a person is suitable for a particular job and a prospective employer relies on your reference letter to their detriment. The prospective employer must prove you have breached a duty of care. Your reference letter can also be construed as misleading or deceptive conduct under the Trade Practices Act where there is no need to prove the duty of care. The moral of the business reference letter is to bear in mind that somebody relying on what you have said about a person can sue and you may need to provide evidence to support the opinion you have expressed.

Another reason for care in providing a reference letter to an ex-employee or colleague is that the person can use the reference to argue wrongful dismissal in the industrial courts. This is a common problem where a person's employment is terminated for reasons of poor performance or misconduct. You can give a person a reference letter with the best will in the world to assist them in their search for another job, only to find you must explain the favourable reference in the context of dismissing the person. This reason alone explains the increasing reluctance in Australia to provide a glowing reference to an ex-employee.

Even a damning reference can get you into trouble. In the English case of *Spring v Guardian Assurance* the House of Lords considered a reference letter issued to a person who lost his job following the restructure of his employer. Mr Spring was an insurance salesman and his employer was taken over by Guardian Assurance. When asked about Mr Spring's work, the former employer told Guardian Assurance in a letter that 'his former superior has further stated that he is a man of little or no integrity and could not be regarded as honest'. The House of Lords ruled that the statement was untrue and the employer breached its duty of care to Mr Spring. It made no difference that Mr Spring was a company representative and not an employee.

The general principle is you need to be in a position to back up what you say about a person in a reference letter. I do not suggest abandoning altogether the practice of giving references—particularly reference letters in business—as this could damage your prospects of securing good employees. You are not expected to give absolute guarantees about what you say in a reference letter, but simply to take reasonable care that the information in the reference can be verified. Problems will usually be avoided if you establish protocols in your organisation as to who provides references and the guidelines for what is to be said about a person. You are entitled to express a frank and honest opinion about a person in a reference letter, but you also need to check that what you say is accurate and reliable. Letter 15.2 may be a useful guide.

15.2 Business reference letter

To whom it may concern

Janet Staples has been in our employ for the past two years, having joined us on graduating from the Horizon Business College. Her duties initially were confined to answering the telephone and typing standard insurance assessment forms.

Janet showed an unusual amount of initiative for a young person and soon acquired skills in programming and operating our Smithson S.E. Computer. She is now proficient in the essential functions of this machine, having programmed the whole of our routine insurance business.

Janet has a pleasant personality and she has been a great asset to us in dealing with customers who often call at our office to take out insurance policies and lodge claim forms. She always checks paperwork accurately and customers have often expressed their satisfaction at the care and attention she gives to her work.

We are indeed sorry to lose Janet's services, but she leaves us to find a position with greater opportunities for advancement. Unfortunately Low Profile Insurance Services is a small company with limited prospects for talented employees. We know that Janet will do well at any task she undertakes, and we wish her every success in the future.

Yours sincerely,
Low Profile Insurance Services

Jack Staid

Jack Staid
General Manager

Letters of congratulations

Printed greeting cards are notorious for saying everything except what you would say yourself. You may wonder about the sincerity of adapting something I have said, but you might have said the same thing yourself had you thought about it long enough— more than you could say for the printed greeting card. Try Letters 15.3 to 15.6 as a starting point.

15.3   Congratulations letter A

I was extremely pleased to learn of your appointment to the Northern Territory government. You did well and I hope the reference was of some help.

I shall follow your future career with great interest and I expect you will soon be Chief Minister. Make sure you get rid of mandatory sentencing laws without delay.

15.4 Congratulations letter B

Congratulations on the birth of your baby daughter. I was delighted when I heard the news. The family must be enjoying her immensely and I hope you are all well.

I look forward to seeing you in the near future—as soon as the new member of the family settles in. As always, I will bring the champagne.

15.5 Congratulations letter C

I heard on the grapevine about your new job and I want to say how pleased I am that your talents have been recognised at last. You deserve the job and nobody is better suited to it than you.

When you have settled in I would like to visit you and find out first-hand how you are getting on. In the meantime, my thoughts/prayers are with you, and I know you can meet any challenge. Fight the good fight!

15.6 Congratulations letter D

Congratulations on your engagement/wedding/anniversary. It is a significant milestone and I hope you enjoy many [more] happy years together.

For my part I am still flying solo, but it is comforting to know you two are [still] together. Keep up the good work for all of us.

Letters of condolence

When somebody you know suffers the loss of a friend or family member, you will want to send a short letter of condolence, or perhaps you might prefer a blank greeting card to write a message of sympathy. As with any other letter, focus on the needs of your reader, and avoid going on about your own loss and despair. Do not say 'I know how you must feel' or 'You must feel as I did when Charlie died'. Grief is an intensely personal experience and nobody should presume to know how another person is feeling. At various stages in the grieving process the person will feel anger, shock, depression and guilt. But this is quite normal. Under no circumstances should you tell someone to 'Move on' or 'Put it behind you'. Your short letter or handwritten greeting card will help a friend or acquaintance get through their ordeal. Letters 15.7 to 15.10 may be a good place to start.

15.7 Condolence letter A

It was a great shock to hear of Tom's death. Only last month we were skiing and he was so fit and healthy. It seems impossible that illness/tragedy should strike him down so quickly, in the prime of his life.

He was a great friend to me and my heart goes out to you at this time. You are in my thoughts/prayers and I am anxious to do anything I can to help you.

15.8 Condolence letter B

I was sorry to hear of your mother's death. She was a fine woman and many of us owe her a great deal.

My thoughts/prayers are with you at this time and I will call you in a few days to see what assistance I can give the family.

15.9 Condolence letter C

Please accept my deepest sympathy for the loss of your father. He was courageous to the end but his illness has been difficult for you during the last few months.

When the time is right I hope we can get away and spend some time together. I still have fond memories of the last time we travelled up the coast.

15.10 Condolence letter D

I was greatly saddened to learn of Mary's death. The joy she brought to others is difficult to describe and you must miss her very much.

The attached poem/song was written as a small token of my gratitude for Mary's life and you may wish to read/sing it at the funeral.

Avoid sending a poem or song if it is your first attempt at verse—you want to ease the pain of the person you are writing to, not add to it! Sending flowers is a useful way to express your sorrow, and a handwritten note or card attached to the flowers will be a thoughtful gesture, although it is not always possible unless your correspondent lives nearby. Flower companies have agents in most cities which will write out or type your message and attach it to the flowers—not quite the same as doing it yourself but the next best thing.

TO GET YOUR NAME IN YOU MIGHT HAVE TO WAIT FOR THE DEATH NOTICES

Responding to letters of condolence is usually a distressing task and you may find it easier to have a plain white card especially printed with an appropriate message. Letter 15.11 may assist.

15.11   Condolence response A

> The family of the late
> [*name of person*]
> acknowledges with gratitude your kind
> thoughts, deeds and expressions of
> sympathy in the loss of a dearly loved
> husband, father and grandfather.
> [*date of death*]

If you feel up to it, a personal note in response to condolences and letters of sympathy is preferable to the printed card. A handwritten note will convey much more than the card even if you write the same message of gratitude to each of your correspondents. By all means use a printed card—perhaps a small testimony to the person who has died—but add your own handwritten words of thanks if you can manage it. Failing that, have a relative or close friend write the note for you. Letter 15.12 may be a useful guide.

15.12   Condolence response B

Don asked me to thank you for your kind words/gift and the beautiful flowers you sent following Tina's death. You helped Don get through a very difficult time and I hope he will be able to thank you himself when he is back on deck.

Letters of invitation and reply

Generally speaking formal invitations are written in the third person and informal invitations in the first person. Any book on etiquette will tell you that a formal invitation is handwritten on white card or plain paper. This may be good advice if you are hosting a small function for just a few people, but otherwise printed cards or printed personal stationery is appropriate. Include the required dress for the function in the lower right-hand corner and the method of responding to the invitation in the lower left-hand corner. If you are hosting a business function always check available dates with your key guests at least three months in advance. Immediately confirm their availability in writing and follow up with the formal invitation as soon as possible. For an engagement with just one person you might get away with a few days' notice. Letter 15.13 covers the invitation and Letters 15.14 and 15.15 are the replies.

15.13   Formal invitation letter

Mr John Smith requests the pleasure of Mrs Joan Brown's company on Saturday 28 July at 6.00 p.m. at the Jubilee Room, Parliament House, Macquarie Street, Sydney.

[Cocktails/supper, etc.]

RSVP: Tel 9230 2111   Dress: Lounge suit
       Friday 20 July   Day dress

15.14   Formal reply A

Mrs Joan Brown accepts with pleasure the kind invitation of Mr John Smith for Saturday 28 July at 6.00 p.m. at the Jubilee Room, Parliament House, Macquarie Street, Sydney.

15.15   Formal reply B

Mrs Joan Brown very much regrets that a previous engagement prevents her accepting the kind invitation of Mr John Smith for Saturday 28 July at 6.00 p.m. at the Jubilee Room, Parliament House, Macquarie Street, Sydney.

If you receive an invitation written in the first person, such as a wedding invitation, you would normally reply using the same language. For example, the invitation may say: 'You are invited to celebrate with us the wedding of Lucy and John.' The appropriate reply would be: 'I will be delighted to celebrate with you Lucy and John's wedding.' The rules for replying to informal invitations are even more flexible although you should follow the language of the invitation as closely as possible. Informal invitations are frequently designed with the assistance of popular graphics and desktop publishing programs. Stick with the first person if you are in any doubt about how to reply. Letters 15.16, 15.17 and 15.18 may assist you with informal invitation letters and replies.

15.16 Informal invitation letter

Mary and I have decided to throw a party at the pier when Mum leaves for her cruise to Noumea. The Overseas Passenger Terminal has a new restaurant upstairs called Sailors and I have booked for lunch next Sunday at 12.30 p.m.

All the family will be there and Mary and I hope you can join us. Mum will certainly appreciate your company—you always manage to lift her spirits. And of course we would all love to see you again.

15.17 Informal reply A

Thank you so much for your kind invitation to join you and Mary for lunch at Sailors next Sunday at 12.30 p.m. at the Overseas Passenger Terminal.

I will be delighted to join the party and to help despatch your mother in good spirits.

15.18 Informal reply B

Thank you so much for your kind invitation to join you and Mary for lunch at Sailors next Sunday at 12.30 p.m. at the Overseas Passenger Terminal. Unfortunately I am leaving for the north coast tomorrow and I will be unable to attend.

I shall call your mother tonight and express my good wishes for the trip. Perhaps we can catch up on her return as I do miss those family get togethers when you all behave so outrageously. Good luck on Sunday.

Letters to dissatisfied customers

In private industry the customer is always right. If customers are dissatisfied, you may have misquoted or mistreated them, or mismanaged, or misunderstood the nature of your business. Always attempt to mend the fence when you fall out with a customer as the problem will only visit you again until you deal with it. Keep in mind the Buddhist truism that the lessons become more gross the longer it takes to learn them. Give yourself a few days to cool off and then write the appropriate letter. Over the years I have used Letters 15.19 to 15.22 to help resolve difficult situations with customers.

15.19 Service provider's letter A

I regret that a misunderstanding has arisen about your account and I accept full responsibility for not properly informing you of the cost of my services. In the circumstances I will accept your cheque for $1200 in full payment of the amount due.

15.20 Service provider's letter B

I am concerned that a mix-up has occurred about the date on which I was expected to complete your job. I have now secured the materials I need to finish the work within seven days and I apologise for any inconvenience caused.

15.21   Service provider's letter C

I am informed you have been mistreated by a member of my staff and I would be grateful if you could call at my office to discuss the situation. Needless to say I am anxious to hear your account of the incident before deciding what to do.

15.22   Service provider's letter D

I failed to attend last night's meeting for which I most sincerely apologise. Matters beyond my control made it impossible to keep the appointment and I was unable to contact you to make alternative arrangements.

As a service provider you will want to be conciliatory with your customers in just about every situation that arises. If you are a manufacturer of goods, however, you need to be rather more circumspect when writing to dissatisfied customers, particularly if they are concerned about whether goods are merchantable or suitable for their intended purpose. For example, your customer may have ordered one kind of product and received another. Once you write and apologise for the error you are immediately responsible in the sense that you have admitted liability for your mistake. Not only must you satisfy the customer's original order but you must compensate the customer for any loss. So long as you are willing to take full responsibility for what you say, Letter 15.23 may assist you with an unhappy customer.

15.23   Manufacturer's letter to customer

Ms A. R. Dent
General Manager
Dynamic Sales Training
644 Conquest Drive
MOTIVATION CITY STA 26844

Dear Ms Dent,

We refer to our discussion last week when you informed us that our motivation video 'Seven Ways to Better Sales Figures' was supposed to be presented to your Monday sales class. Instead the class was shocked to see our alternative lifestyle video, 'Seven Ways to Nirvana'.

This unfortunate error occurred as a result of a mistake in our packaging department. You will appreciate that we package hundreds of video movies every day, and the similarity in the two titles led to the mix-up.

We have questioned the employee responsible and we believe that an honest mistake was made. The person has an excellent record with the company and no possibility exists that you were deliberately sent the wrong video.

It may be difficult to assess your loss as a result of the error, but certainly we would be willing to meet the cost of reconvening your Monday sales class. You may also be interested in the enclosed complimentary copy of our new title, 'Ways to Suppress Anger'.

Yours sincerely,
Haphazard Video Sales

H Hazard

H. Hazard (Mr)
General Manager

Marketing and sales letters

Recently I had the good fortune to visit the offices of Reader's Digest in Sydney and I asked about the success of the company's sales letters. I was intrigued because I had received a business letter from the company a few weeks earlier and it was as dreary as you can imagine when compared to their standard fare sales letter. On closer examination, however, the business letter had the four key features I mentioned at the beginning of the book—person, issue, purpose and action—and proof that it worked was my presence at the Reader's Digest offices. I had complained to the company about privacy, as well as a report that rated politicians the least credible of any professionals, and I had been invited to discuss my concerns personally. From Reader's Digest I learned that sales letters depend for their success on how they look as much as what they say. All the rules about effective letter writing still apply, but the sales letter includes CAPITAL letters, words and phrases underlined for emphasis, words in **bold type**, hand-written notes in the margin, quotes, question marks, *italics*, and so on. With the benefit of this information—and using the WriteQuick program—I drafted Letter 15.24 (on the following page) as a sample sales letter.

My sample sales and marketing letter is a bit busy and you do need to be careful about too much emphasis and variety. Some people go right over the top in their enthusiasm for their products and services with asterisks, boxes, headings and exclamation marks. Use these devices at your peril because generally only the marketing experts know when they work. On the other hand, if you are using a letter to cold canvass a prospective customer you need to make a visual impact. Note that the sample letter is addressed 'Dear Reader' which runs against everything I have said about direct mail and targeting your market. Large mailing houses might get away with a general 'Dear Reader' mailout, but you and I could do it only on a local basis where we might be recognised as an integral part of the product or service we are hoping to sell. If you are selling into a foreign market you definitely need to identify the person you are writing to and follow up with a personal presentation. Letter 15.25 may be a useful guide, particularly if you are involved in manufacturing.

Widget Card

123 Sydney Road, Sydney, NSW 2000, Australia
Tel: 1800 000 000 Fax: 1800 000 000
ABN 80 000 000 000 www.widgetcard.com

LIGHT YEARS AHEAD IN PLASTIC

'The light went on for me from the moment I started using Widget Card.'
S. O. Famous

Dear Reader,

You are invited to test the latest money-saving consumer service FREE for six months.

For the next six months, you will have instant access through your automatic teller machine to the lowest prices in Australia using the award-winning WIDGET CARD.

HERE'S HOW IT WORKS TO SAVE YOU $$$s ON JUST ABOUT EVERYTHING YOU WANT TO BUY.

What would you like to buy over the next six months? Clothes and jewellery? Furniture? New sound equipment? What about a new flat-screen television, or the latest home computer? Perhaps you're intending to travel in the near future?

By all means shop around—department stores, shopping centres, corner stores . . . even your local trash and treasure market. When you find what you want, the first thing you always worry about is the price . . . but not anymore.

SIMPLY ASK YOUR RETAILER TO SWIPE YOUR WIDGET CARD OVER THE BARCODE OF WHATEVER IT IS YOU WANT TO BUY . . . AND THEN INSERT THE WIDGET CARD IN YOUR NEAREST AUTOMATIC TELLER MACHINE.

Your bank will have one of its friendly computers on standby, ready to check your retailer's price against other prices in the area.

What you want to buy might be on sale right across the road—at half the price you were about to pay. You could save big dollars over the next six months.

HOW DO YOU GET YOUR FREE WIDGET CARD?

Just call me today and answer a few simple questions to tell the bank whether you're rich or poor. If you answer correctly I promise to despatch your WIDGET CARD in the very next post—no delay, no fuss.

Yours sincerely,
WIDGET CARD SERVICES

B Light

B. Light (Mr)
Regional Manager
Competition and Consumer Division

P.S. Why not get an extra WIDGET CARD for a friend or family member?

15.25   Overseas marketing letter

Mr Guang Ho
General Manager
Ho Lee Distribution Company
276 New Territory Highway
KOWLOON HK 27600

Dear Mr Ho,

We are the manufacturers in Australia of an exclusive range of high-quality leathergoods and we are taking the liberty of enclosing our latest product brochure together with complimentary samples of our products. These products may be familiar to you as they are available in 22 countries throughout the world.

David Wang of the Hong Kong Trade Centre suggested we contact you on the basis that you are the wholesalers and distributors for the Eastern Department Stores. We ask that you consider our range of products. We could deliver in Hong Kong, four weeks after an order is placed, the following quantities at the prices listed:

    2000 wallets @ $49.00 each
    2000 cardholders @ $32.00 each
    2000 handbags @ $74.00 each
    2000 purses @ $56.00 each
    2000 keyholders @ $28.00 each

Prices quoted are in Australian dollars. Larger orders would result in a lower unit cost, which we would be pleased to quote on request.

Our representative, Mr Tom Smith, will be in Hong Kong later this month, and with your permission, he will call and discuss our product range in greater detail.

Yours sincerely,
Kangaroo Leather Company

B . Red

B. Red (Mr)
General Manager

If you can expand your business to include some overseas activity, you will enjoy the luxury of claiming your overseas trip as a taxation deduction. More importantly, you will have the opportunity to look more closely at the way people overseas do business. You will have greater access to otherwise foreign business activities, and inevitably you will change the way you do business back home. There is every reason to be optimistic about market prospects in Asia, for example. A few years ago I was browsing through Wing On department store in Hong Kong and I came across a boutique selling high-class women's fashions. You guessed it—they were made in Australia. High-quality, low-volume industries will always find a market for their products.

Travel and holiday letters

Sometimes things can go wrong on a holiday or business trip. Accommodation may be inferior to that which was promised, you might be expected to pay for accommodation or other services when you were informed that the trip was all-inclusive, or you may find that a holiday package that was supposed to include certain features does not. In these cases you should complain to the tour operator's local representative or your hotel manager in the host country (not too loudly), and you should take the matter up with your travel agent when you return home. Letter 15.26 may prompt you to put pen to paper.

15.26 Travel company letter A

Mr Wally World
General Manager
Big Trip Travel Company
254 Leisure Drive
HOLIDAY PARK STA 22700

Dear Wally,

Last week I returned from my fourteen-day Jetpack Tour of Hong Kong and, as you know, a number of unsatisfactory incidents occurred during the trip:

1. Although my itinerary clearly stated that the tour was booked at the High Point Hotel, accommodation was provided at the Low Point Hotel, an inferior establishment.
2. The tour was to include a day trip to Macau, and instead I was conducted to mainland China where I failed to find any gambling facilities.
3. The sampan trip around Hong Kong Harbour was most unsatisfactory. The vessel collided with a motor launch, throwing me into the harbour.

I would be obliged if you could give the above matters your urgent attention and advise whether you intend paying appropriate compensation.

Yours sincerely,

A Traveller

A. Traveller (Ms)

If the travel agent rejects your complaints, you can complain to the Australian Competition and Consumer Commission (ACCC) or the Australian Federation of Travel Agents (AFTA) in your capital city. It is an offence for a travel agent or tour operator to give false or misleading information about holiday packages and travel arrangements. Travel agents and tour operators may argue that reasonable precautions were taken to ensure that the information provided was accurate or that the problems were due to persons or events beyond their control. Statutory responsibilities vary between different States and Territories and generally the authorities will not order payment of compensation.

To enforce your claim you may need to bring an action in a lower court or the Fair Trading Tribunal, and you must be able to prove damages—the amount of money you have lost as a result of the actions or errors complained of. One of the defences to an action for compensation would certainly be that the tour operators have excluded themselves from liability in the conditions set out in their literature and on the back of tickets. Nevertheless, if there was a serious mishap or error for which the tour operators were responsible, the exclusion clause would not be an effective defence to an action for breach of their duty of care or contractual obligations owed to customers.

Another method of resolving a dispute with a travel agent or tour operator is to go to arbitration. Often the booking conditions in travel literature and on the back of tickets include a provision that any dispute should be resolved by an arbitrator or independent referee. The arbitrator is an impartial and qualified person who attempts to mediate the dispute. Personally I am not a fan of arbitration as you must agree beforehand about who will be responsible for costs and you must agree to be bound by the decision of the arbitrator. You may be able to negotiate with the arbitrator to submit to the process on the basis that you can still go to court or the tribunal if you are unhappy with the decision.

As with other professionals, travel agents and tour operators are required to contribute to a fidelity fund to cover people who are the victims of travel fraud. Each State and Territory operates a Travel Agents' Compensation Fund managed by the government and you are entitled to claim on the fund if you are defrauded of your hard earned cash. Strictly speaking, the fund will not protect you from negligence or mismanagement, but I have known cases where successful claims were made in circumstances where fraud could not be proved. It is worth making a claim in any case where you have parted with your money and the agent has failed to deliver the promised holiday or travel arrangements.

Sometimes you may feel a bit let down at the end of your holiday, even though nobody has defrauded you or acted negligently. You may feel disappointed that the holiday fell short of your expectations. If this is the case, make sure you put pen to paper—travel agents and tour operators operate in a competitive industry, and they will sometimes pay compensation if you state your case clearly. More precisely, the travel company will give you a favourable hearing as a gesture of goodwill. Compensation is really only payable when you have suffered damages in the legal sense. However you describe it, payment for your trouble is one certain way to get your repeat travel business.

On a plane trip from Athens to Sydney, I once met a British accountant who was on his second overseas holiday with an English travel company. His first holiday with the company—a package tour to Barbados in the West Indies—had been a resounding success because of an incident involving compensation. The resort facilities in Barbados were being upgraded during the period of the accountant's holiday, and he was unable to use the swimming pool. He took a photograph of the incapacitated pool and, on his return to England, wrote a complaint letter to the travel company. The accountant received a cheque from the travel company for £350 by return mail. He was kind enough to give me a copy of the letter he wrote to the travel company, and Letter 15.27 is my adaptation of the letter.

15.27   Travel company letter B

Mr Bill Ticket
General Manager
Holiday Camp Travel Company
27 Holiday Boulevard
CHIPCHESTER UK 12451

Dear Bill,

Last week I returned to Chipchester after ten relaxing days on your 'Barbados Escape Tour'. Except for the swimming pool, the facilities at the Barbados Sun Seeker Resort were excellent, and equal to your usual high standard. I am a regular visitor to your holiday camps and I have visited each of your resorts in Spain.

Unfortunately, for the whole of my time at the Barbados resort, extensive repairs were being carried out at the swimming pool and it could not be used. Not only that, but great clouds of dust billowed across the resort during daylight hours as a result of construction work and I had to remain indoors. I am enclosing a photograph showing the extent of the repairs. The brown patches in the photograph are the dust clouds.

It is not my usual nature to complain, but I do feel that the use of a pool is very important to an English tourist who cannot enjoy swimming in England because of the inclement weather. You will also be aware that the swimming pool is featured in your 'Barbados Escape Tour' brochure, and I believe that some form of compensation is in order.

Yours sincerely,

I. N. Dulgent

I. N. Dulgent (Mr)

A few days after I arrived in Sydney, a friend of mine was able to benefit from the experience of the British accountant. My friend had just returned to Australia after a disastrous business trip in the Pacific, where he booked an eight-day package tour with a large travel company at the Le Legon Hotel in Vanuatu. Knowing the flight went via Noumea, he did not think too much about the voucher he received from the travel company, which said 'Le Legon Hotel' on one line and 'Noumea' on another. Unbelievably, there are two Le Legon Hotels—one in Vanuatu and the other in Noumea. My friend spent eight days at the right hotel in the wrong country. He approached his accountant about whether he could claim a tax deduction for a trip to the wrong place, he asked my advice about the possibility of suing and he consulted his doctor about the nervous disorder he had developed from the worry of it all. I suggested a letter to the travel company along the lines of the British accountant's letter and I am pleased

to report that my friend enjoyed the Le Legon Hotel in Vanuatu with the compliments of the travel company. He will still get his tax deduction, his nervous disorder is gone and I hope you will tell your friends about this book.

Postscript

A final word about copyright. You have my express permission to use the text of any of the letters in this book, but I am not responsible for the context in which you use them. Avoid like the plague using other people's letters without their permission— the author of a letter owns the copyright. Using another person's letter in a derogatory way can lead to a claim for damages as you will be reducing the value of the copyright. The letter's author also enjoys moral rights, which protect the form and content of the letter, and these rights were recently made enforceable under Australian law.

You also have my permission to use the letters in the WriteQuick computer program on the same understanding. Some of the letters are available on the Internet at *www.writequick.com* and I will be happy to send you others from the program to deal with specific situations. All you need to do is tell me who you are writing to from the list in Appendix One and what kind of letter you are writing from the list in Appendix Two. If you would like to purchase the WriteQuick program, it is available at *www.writequick.com* or direct from my company:

WriteQuick Software Pty Limited
GPO Box 719, Sydney 2001
Tel: 1800 SCRIBE (1800 727 423)

Good luck with your letter writing and thanks for using my book.

Appendix One

Correspondent type

the complete original letter writing system™

Who are you writing to?

Accountant
Advertiser
Advertising Agency
Airline Operator
Bank Manager
Builder
Business Agent
Club Operator
Comp Soft Designer
Computer Supplier
Corporate Manager
Court Magistrate
Creditor
Customer
Debtor
Defamatory Author
Developer
Direct Mailer
Employee
Employer

Fashion Designer
Financial Adviser
Food Supplier
Government
Hairdresser
Hospital
Hotelier
Insurance Company
Internet Service
Landlord
Lawyer
Local Council
Manufacturer
Medical Officer
Motor Car Dealer
Motor Car Repairer
Musician
Neighbour
Newspaper Editor
Police Officer

Politician
Polluter
Public Servant
Publicist
Radio Broadcaster
Real Estate Agent
Religious Instructor
Repairer
Retailer
School Teacher
Stockbroker
Tax Officer
Telephone Provider
Television Network
Television Presenter
Tenant
Travel Agent
Undertaker
University Professor
Valuer

Appendix Two

Letter type

What kind of letter are you writing?

Acceptance
Acknowledgment
Agreement
Apology
Appointment
Complaint
Complimentary
Condolence
Confirmation
Congratulations
Correction
Declining Invitation
Demand
Donation
Encouragement
Endorsement
Evaluation

Explanation
Follow-up
Friendship
Fundraising
Inquiry
Instruction
Introductory
Invitation
Job Application
Junk Mail
Offer
Personal
Promotional
Query
Reference
Refusal
Regret

Reminder
Reply
Report to Regulator
Reprimand
Request
Resignation
Response
Retraction
Rocket
Sales
Subscription
Support
Survey
Sympathy
Thank you
Work Experience

Bibliography

Armstrong, Mark, Lindsay, David and Watterson, Ray, *Media Law in Australia* (third edition), Oxford University Press, Melbourne, 1999.

Barnsley, Garry, *Letters for Lawyers: Conveyancing*, Federation Press, Sydney, 2000.

Baugh, L. Sue, *Handbook for Practical Letter Writing*, NTC Publishing Group, Chicago, 1991.

Bellemore, Phillipa, *Tenants' Rights Manual* (second edition), Redfern Legal Centre Publishing, Sydney, 1997.

Bird, Drayton, *How to Write Sales Letters that Sell*, Kogan Page Limited, London, 1994.

Breen, Peter, *Advance Australia Fair: Reforming the Legal System with a Rights and Responsibilities Code*, Cape Byron Press, Byron Bay, 2000.

Compton, Tony, *Buying a Small Business*, Wrightbooks, Melbourne, 1999.

Dal Pont, Gino, *Lawyers' Professional Responsibility in Australia and New Zealand*, Law Book Company, Sydney, 1996.

Galligan, Brian and Sampford, Charles (eds), *Rethinking Human Rights*, Federation Press, Sydney, 1997.

Grygel, Joan (ed), *The World Book of Word Power*, World Book Inc., Chicago, 1997.

Hunt, Murray, *Using Human Rights in English Courts*, Hart Publishing, Oxford, 1998.

Janner, Greville, *Janner's Complete Letterwriter* (fourth edition), Century Hutchinson, Sydney, 1989.

Joel, Asher, *Australian Protocol and Procedures*, Angus & Robertson, Sydney, 1988.

MacAdam, Alastair and Pyke, John, *Judicial Reasoning and the Doctrine of Precedent in Australia*, Butterworths, Sydney, 1998.

McAllister, Margaret (ed.), *The Law Handbook* (seventh edition), Redfern Legal Centre Publishing, Sydney, 1999.

O'Neill, Nick and Handley, Robin, *Retreat from Injustice: Human Rights in Australian Law*, Federation Press, Sydney, 1994.

Rayner, Moira, *Rooting Democracy: Growing the Society We Want*, Allen & Unwin, Sydney, 1997.

Susskind, Richard, *The Future of Law: Facing the Challenges of Information Technology*, Oxford University Press, Oxford, 1998.

Thornhill, John, *Making Australia: Exploring our National Conversation*, Millenium Books, Sydney, 1992.

Thornton, Phil, Phelan, Liam and McKeowan, Bill, *I Protest: Fighting for your Rights*, Pluto Press, Sydney, 1997.

Tunstall, Joan, *Better, Faster Email*, Allen & Unwin, Sydney, 1999.

White, Margaret, *Put it in Writing*, Choice Books, Sydney, 1994.

Wienbroer, Diana Roberts, Hughes, Elaine and Silverman, Jay, *Rules of Thumb for Business Writers*, McGraw-Hill, New York, 1998.

Index